Readings

Readings

Acts of Close Reading in Literary Theory

Julian Wolfreys

Edinburgh University Press

To
J. Hillis Miller

© Julian Wolfreys, 2000

Edinburgh University Press Ltd
22 George Square, Edinburgh

Typeset in Bembo and Futura
by Norman Tilley Graphics, Northampton
and printed and bound in Great Britain
by Creative Print and Design, Ebbw Vale, Wales

A CIP record for this book is available from
the British Library

ISBN 0 7486 1352 8 (paperback)

Contents

Preface and Acknowledgements

'Good' literary criticism, the only worthwhile kind, implies an act, a literary signature or counter-signature, an inventive experience of language, *in* language, an inscription of the act of reading in the field of the text that is read.

(Jacques Derrida)

But the step-by-step commentary is of necessity a renewal of the entrances to the text, it avoids structuring the text *excessively*, avoids giving it that additional structure which would come from a dissertation and would close it: it stars the text, instead of assembling it.

(Roland Barthes)

When I picture a perfect reader, I always picture a monster of courage and curiosity, also something supple, cunning, cautious, a born adventurer and discoverer.

(Friedrich Nietzsche)

The meanings of the verb 'to read' are numerous, its origins, appropriately, obscure, as the *Oxford English Dictionary* informs us.[1] Earliest Teutonic and Sanskrit precursors suggest acts of deliberation, consideration, giving thought or attendance to, or otherwise to succeed or to accomplish. Later definitions complicate matters. To read 'read' necessarily dictates the necessity of being open to receiving numerous significations, a complex web of possible meanings, a skein of traces and inscriptions within the single – and singular – word. In order to be able to begin reading what it means to read, one must open oneself to the idea that what is read is only a momentary recognition. It is perhaps a fleeting response to a certain pulse or rhythm. In order to stabilise that act of reading, one must perform the reading with a degree of violence, even while, and as the corollary of such violence, what is read is never wholly read. Something remains, something is left behind, something is missed altogether, something other is still yet to be read.

There is the rare and obscure transitive use of the verb. It can mean to think, suppose, or have an idea, to guess or otherwise extrapolate by conjecture or speculation. Equally rare is the idea that reading involves an act of taking *for* something, to discover the meaning and to transmit to another. Slightly more familiar is the notion of reading as prediction, of foretelling or foreseeing, discerning or distinguishing. Reading thus involves assigning textual traces a future possibility.

The sense of inspection and interpretation is relatively common. This leads to that sense of reading where a meaning or significance is attached to an object. Yet reading can also mean to leave a mark or otherwise impress onto something, such as a fabric or page, an imprint. Thus, while the sense of reading may in some cases attempt to be predictive, in many others, reading is determined as the response to the sign or the trace, to some manifestation of the other, though never the other itself. Reading is an act of decoding something which has been left behind from the past. There is always a question of temporality in the act of reading, in both the performative event, the encounter with the text, and in the processes by which the text is assembled. The structure to be read is not only spatial and rhythmic; it is also temporal and polyvalent. It is, perhaps, excessive, beyond all polyvalence.[2]

An even more obscure meaning for this word 'read' is in its use not as a verb, but as a noun, signifying the stomach of an animal: the belly of the beast no less. This sense, the *Oxford English Dictionary* tentatively speculates – or *reads* – as being possibly the oldest of meanings and uses, older than those other senses already given above, in the opening paragraph. Such a meaning estranges for us the use of the word 'read' quite forcibly. Can we speculate a possible connection between the stomach material and the act of interpretation? Can we read 'read' and 'read', reading between them a silent passage? How can we 'hear' the difference in looking at the inscribed sign? Or can we read there the attempted act of communication on the part of the one who reads for others, the earliest form of exegete or scholar, the one who combines discernment and prediction? Is there in this process, not an act of communication as reading, so much as the desire for one? With that movement, is there discernible the concomitant opening – inevitably – of an aporia between the 'read' (of the animal) and the 'reading', between the 'reading' and what is 'read'? It is in this space that readers find themselves, placed via the event of reading within the body of the text to be deciphered. The reader replaces the *reads* with the act of reading, as though the act of communication involves displacement, substitution, transference.

At the same time, it is necessary to seek ways of activating the difference. In order to find the appropriate metaphor or figure of catachresis for acts of critical reading, to think about reading differently, what, in the performance of critical reading, might be understood through this figure of the 'reads'? Perhaps – we suggest this provisionally and with the greatest caution – citation itself.[3] Citation is nothing other than the removal by force from the textual body that bodily fragment which, in being transplanted into the critical reading, allows for a somewhat *intestinal* connection. What we want to suggest – with regard to the present consideration of reading – is that, beginning again and again with citation, we seek through the double motion of incision and excision, to open reading to itself. We attempt to place the *reads* on the table as it were, in the attempt to come closer to acts of reading. At the same time, however, we have also to acknowledge how the opening of the textual body remains.

This opening or staging of the aporetic experience in reading is precisely the moment of appearing to want to decide on the undecidable. Such an instance invokes the temporary suspension of reading. With it comes that moment of not reading, which, far from being readable as suggesting that everything is up for grabs, that nothing means anything, or that because everything can mean anything nothing means nothing, is in fact the spur to response and responsibility. In the face of the undecidable, what remains except the reading of remains? What remains except the response and, with that, the responsibility, to continue reading? In Beckettian fashion, unable to go on, we go on, the moment of the reading being the retreating horizon towards which we attempt to read. We are, furthermore, left with the responsibility which undecidability imposes upon us. We must respond by seeking to be the good reader, as Hillis Miller puts it, rather than the bad reader, whom Derrida defines, perhaps for the first time in *The Post Card* (1980).

The bad reader (whom Derrida admits to loving, by the way) is the one who rushes with indecent, even journalistic haste, to decision, to decide on a reading, and thereby to have done with reading, once and for all. Bearing this in mind, and seeking all the while to avoid becoming the bad reader, to have the last word or to close the book on reading, how do we read so as to avoid having read? How do we learn to read patiently, rigorously, in such a manner that we know all the while that we have not yet read, we have not yet done (with) reading, that the clews, the entrails remain as the unread, the not (yet) read, as the constantly receding horizon on which our desire as readers focuses? Perhaps what this means is that, as Harold Bloom suggests, all that we can do is practise acts of strong reading which will be, inevitably, misreadings. Once more we find ourselves confronted with the possibility of violence (see, for example, the citation below from Slavoj Žižek) as part of the very condition of reading, a violence left over from the days when, going on 'gut' impulses perhaps, those who were appointed as readers lugged the guts or wrenched the *reads* from the dying or dead animal. Reading as dismemberment. Is this not what we do each time when we perform an act of so-called 'close reading'?

It is perhaps the case, therefore, that all our more common ideas concerning what it means, 'to read', may have developed in some lost moment from the determination on the part of lost peoples to prognosticate, discern, or otherwise interpret good and bad fortune, by perusing (another meaning) the innards of animals. Certainly Shakespeare offers this image in *Julius Caesar*. Caesar is warned not to leave his house by the 'augurers':

> *Servant:* They would not have you stir forth today.
> Plucking the entrails of an offering forth,
> They could not find a heart within the beast.
>
> (*Julius Caesar* 2.2.37–40)[4]

The moment is interestingly convoluted. The reading – constituted as a prohibition – comes about as a result of not being able to read the future fully. While the 'reads' are plucked out, the heart is missing. Unable to conduct the reading in the proper manner, Caesar's prognosticators deliver a reading which speaks of the impossibility of completing a reading, while also attempting a partial reading. There is a complex transaction at work here between reading and its impossibility.

Reading, therefore, is always – always already – connected with some mystical or perhaps telepathic possibility,[5] with the desire to translate in ways which are not reducible to matters of logic or rationality, so as to make sense of events or, in some other fashion, make sense of events yet to occur. The question of multiple temporalities conjoint in a single moment is complex, and paradoxical. To reiterate, the suggestion is one of transference. The read of the slaughtered creature becomes, through consideration on the part of the appointed expert, the one who keeps the significance of the signs a secret, transposed onto the mind, into the discourse of that self-same expert, which is then, subsequently, passed on to the rest of the community, digested, regurgitated, disseminated. The read of the animal passes into the reading of the shaman. The material of the innards is internalised in the mind, and made palatable – translated in some manner – for the consumption on the part of others. All subsequent acts of reading therefore seek to retrace the traceries of veins, arteries, vessels and other means of communicative tissue in the form of textile, textured, exegesis. And that we term this exegesis suggests, through its classical form, that we wish to rationalise and distance ourselves from the moment of psychic consumption. The grotesque, corporeal aspect of reading is cleaned up, the act aestheticised, given a refiguration in a clean light. Yet in reading there is still, always, regurgitation. In our acts of reading, research comes back via the bodily ruins we call citations.

The essay which follows considers single moments in the act of reading.

It does not explore entire readings, tracing patiently the contours of every text. I am not therefore claiming to read or to have read any of the other critics, philosophers, or theorists whose texts have been interrupted and which, then, return in ruins. Nor is this a series of readings of the 'concepts', 'paraconcepts', or 'keywords' which the reader will find aligned against the proper names on the contents page of this volume. These terms name the possibility of thinking reading differently, and have imposed themselves on me in the process of writing.

The attempt is to consider, with that necessary and inescapable degree of violence already mentioned, a series of distinct figures of reading. Reading the trope of reading as it surfaces in passing in particular chapters, articles and books, the following essay – composed of a number of essays, the identities of which are not necessarily distinct – pauses at or before articulations of the limits to which reading goes. Everywhere, yet in highly different ways and overdetermined contexts, there is to be found reading at work which pushes at the limit of the analytical act, and which also seeks to negotiate the double limit of the readable and the unreadable. The interruption of the interpretive rhythm occurs the moment reading is brought to light, given voice in numerous places, and unveiled in the reflexive regard given the interpretive or analytical act.

The essay draws on the work of critics who for the most part are often conveniently and hastily gathered under the heading of 'poststructuralism' (in order, we would suggest, to avoid the effort of reading). This is not a definition, much less a *reading*, which I necessarily accept. The extracts chosen for this book come from this conventionally defined corpus because, despite the claims of those antipathetic to critical thinking and critical or literary theory, what we can read across such texts is an insistent and noticeable return to the question of what it means to read, as part of the process of reading itself. Often it is the case that those who accuse so-called 'poststructuralists' of bad reading are nothing more nor less than bad readers themselves, in the Derridean sense, indulging in what Geoffrey Bennington (in the extract from his '*Inter*' (1999)) calls 'a sort of intellectual journalism'. Or, what is worse, all too frequently, there are those who criticise various acts of rigorous, patient, and often generous reading, who clearly have not read at all. Yet, despite the all too frequent and predictable claims that Derrida, Althusser, Kristeva, Foucault, De Man, Bloom, et al. are *bad* readers, what may be read in their texts is nothing other than a constant interest in the act of reading, expressed in countless, differing ways. I would even go so far as to say that the critics and philosophers gathered here are always engaged in acts of close reading, often of the most intimate and patient kind.

In choosing the fragments, ruins, citations, and extracts which follow,

I am not interested in situating these excursions into the rhythms of a reading as some form of direct or oppositional polemic to the charges of bad reading. What I seek to respond to is the singularity of these ruined texts, and that singularity which is pursued in these fragments in the texts of others. The essays are not, this essay is not, organised by any governing thesis, nor does this volume assume common ground between the extracts. There is no attempt here to form or forge a family atmosphere or resemblance. Indeed, the only common thread between the texts, and those in whose names they appear, is the attention to the folds of reading.

This is, no doubt, to suggest a reading, to impose a limit, however slight, despite my desire to resist any governing argument. However, rather than reading this as a thesis, I hope that this provisional identification may, in itself, be read as a response, dictated by my own understanding of the responsibility owed to reading and to the text of the other. Furthermore, and as part of the undertaking to avoid programming effects, there is neither a conscious attempt to extrapolate from the particular to the general, nor the effort to make a case for, say, 'the thought of Jacques Derrida' from the exploration of a single statement. Each response in this essay seeks to provide a phatic image or snapshot of the turn to reading, and reading's various unexpected turns. The responses which situate loosely the various essays in relation to each other, and which are part of the overall weave of this text, are generated by the understanding that reading must always begin *again*, repeatedly, in response to the other, while recognising in the response and as the responsibility that reading imposes on us, that reading is never completed.

I would like to thank the following, for suggestions, encouragement, or comments on parts or all of this book: Mark Currie, Antony Easthope, SunHee Kim Gertz, Peggy Kamuf, Jim Kincaid, Peter Manning, J. Hillis Miller, Jean-Michel Rabaté, Ruth Robbins, Nicholas Royle, Margaret Russett, Ken Womack. I would also like to thank Carissa Lamas for her invaluable editorial assistance. I would like to thank the students in my modern literary criticism and theory class at the University of Southern California who were willing to explore the stranger twists and turns of reading with me. Thanks are due to Kara Kalenius for reading and commenting, despite being already overwhelmed with reading matter, and I would like to thank Jackie Dylla, who made it possible for me to write, quite literally. I would also like to thank Rita Winter whose attentive and diligent copy-editing was invaluable. At Edinburgh University Press, James Dale and Jackie Jones have been of immense help, and, as ever, it has been a real pleasure to work with them.

Constructions, Citations, Fragments, *Remaniements*

But as there is no such thing as an innocent reading, we must say what reading we are guilty of.

We were all philosophers. We did not read *Capital* as economists, as historians or as philologists ... We read *Capital* as philosophers, and therefore posed it a different question ... we posed it the question of its *relation to its object*, hence both the question of the specificity of its *object*, and the question of the specificity of its *relation* to that object, i.e., the question of the nature of the type of discourse set to work to handle this object, the question of scientific discourse. And since there can never be a definition without a difference, we posed *Capital* the question of the specific difference both of its object and its discourse ...
[...]
To read *Capital* as philosophers is precisely to question the specific object of a specific discourse, and the specific relationship between this discourse and its object; it is therefore to put to the *discourse–object* unity the question of the epistemological status which distinguishes this particular unity from other forms of discourse–object unity. Only this reading can determine the answer to a question that concerns the place *Capital* occupies in the history of knowledge.
[...]
Hence a philosophical reading of *Capital* is quite the opposite of an innocent reading. It is a guilty reading, but not one that absolves its crime on confessing it. On the contrary, it takes the responsibility for its crime as a 'justified crime' and defends it by proving its necessity. It is therefore a special reading which exculpates itself as a reading by posing every guilty reading the very question that unmasks its innocence, the mere question of its innocence: *what is it to read?*

Louis Althusser, 'From *Capital* to Marx's Philosophy',
Reading Capital (1979, 14–15)

What is it to read?

How are we to answer this question? Is it answerable? Will we have done with it at the end of this essay? The very difficulty of answering lies in the apparent simplicity, the naked transparency of this question. All at once, it appears readable and yet, for all that, remains to be read, if not unreadable. We cannot escape this problem.

The year 1968 seems like a good year from which to begin, and to which to return, if we are to speak of the question of reading, and to talk about this act of reading, moreover, which does not assume itself to be innocent. Indeed, it appears desirable, if not necessary, as an introductory polemical gesture or opening gambit – as a means of seeking to read reading – to state that guilty reading 'began' in the year in which *Reading Capital* was published, even though it has been suggested that a more significant moment of which a kind of reading was the product was not, in fact, this year at all. Rather, another provisional starting point might be the Algerian War of Independence.[1]

That is not true, of course, strictly speaking. It is neither true nor not true. As a statement concerning the beginning of reading, it is at least guilty of a kind of rhetorical manipulation in the interests of reading differently, so to speak. But, then, neither is the statement with which we began true, absolutely. However, these appear to be readings, of sorts, even if they avoid reading or acknowledge, indirectly, that reading is deferred. They might perhaps be 'strong readings', if this phrase is read as suggesting that they are not readings at all, but are, instead, statements which are keen to present a position, regardless of reading.[2] If they have any virtue, these two statements at least present the possibility of a spacing of 'beginning-to-read'. No single origin, therefore.

This is still a guilty act. We have just admitted as much, though not in so many words. And guilt, the admission, and the concomitant question of responsibility implicated in any guilty act, is also an appropriate place from where to start, even if the moment of introduction is both a double gesture, a deferral, and an excuse.

Nevertheless, one has to begin somewhere, perhaps where one always begins, in the folds of a citation.[3]

Rather, say, perhaps, that we begin, before beginning, with an interruption (an interruption in the 'history' of reading, or reading (as) a history of interruptions?), this being one possible acknowledgement of responsibility in relation to the fragment with which we have chosen to begin.

Beginning, then, with Louis Althusser, beginning also with the question of guilty reading, we note that Althusser returns to Marx, to the question of reading Marx, specifically *Capital*, in a particular way, so as to move beyond other ways of reading – as a philosopher. Nothing could be clearer, and yet, at the same time, such a statement of guilt articulates another question: what does it mean to read *as a philosopher*? To read this phrase, *reading as a philosopher*, is at once all too easy and impossible. Indeed, it seems so straightforward that it is not read at all. Thinking we know what it means, we pass over it without question, without reading. Yet, Althusser confesses – *mea culpa* – to engaging in an interested act of reading, and proceeds to explain what exactly such an interest, such a responsibility, entails.

In this act of confession, however, Althusser acknowledges that which cannot be avoided, *if there is no such thing as an innocent reading*. No one who reads is innocent, even though the assumption of innocence is undoubtedly assumed on the part of some. In order to comprehend what it means to read as a philosopher, it is therefore necessary, ignoring any institutional or professional determination, or culturally conventional definition (an innocent reading?) of what a philosopher is, to suggest what might comprise this 'innocent' reading, at least on the evidence presented by Althusser.

Reading as a philosopher in this local instance – the guilty reading – is opposed to other readings: those of the economist, the historian, the philologist. Such innocent approaches to the text do not necessarily read at all. That is to say, their relationship to the text is technical, mechanical even, exploitative. They mine the text of *Capital*, extracting from it that which can be used, put to work in a profitable fashion. Meaning thus becomes use-value, the text reduced to the restricted economy of the thematic reading process   *operating according to principles, postulates, axioms or definitions, and proceeding along the discursive lines of a linear order of reasons*   in such a process, the reading is, in a curious, violent and peremptory fashion, concluded before it has got underway.[4] We might even suggest that there is no reading at all, so innocent is this procedure.

On the other hand, to read as a philosopher, we would hesitatingly and provisionally propose, would be to read not so as to extract a use-value or commodity from the text, or to treat the text as a commodity, parts of which can be used up, leaving only waste. Rather, it would be to activate the text epistemologically within the history of thought. Such a reading, the guilty act of which Althusser speaks, is, strictly speaking, technological neither in method nor intent. Instead, reading mobilises the text within a field of forces which are, in part, if not historical, then 'historial', and to which the text belongs. Yet the reading is guilty, precisely because it takes responsibility for the very question of historicity, which innocent reading would ignore. Whether or not Althusser achieves this is not the question here.[5] The question of what Althusser achieves is not at stake, because the immediate concern in following the Althusserian fragment is not with a reading of Althusser's text. Instead, the interest here, as elsewhere through-out this essay, is with *reading*, with questions of reading differently. This is not a reading of Althusser, so much as it is a strategic opening of reading, in itself and to itself, from, let us say, the other of reading (which is not, of course, not reading). The Althusserian fragment provides the occasion, not the object of such a procedure. It is enough, as a place from which to begin, to understand how, in positioning this act of 'reading as a philos-opher' strategically, his gesture opens for us the means to read differently, to interrupt reading from some other place, as a sign of the responsibility that accompanies every act of reading, and yet which is overlooked.

Hence a philosophical reading, provisionally defined, is one which, in seeking to begin reading a particular text, makes it possible for the reading to be turned back on itself. In instituting any act of reading, the question must always be asked: *what is it to read?* Reading must ask this of itself in the act of the 'philosophical' movement of self-reflection, as Althusser makes apparent. Furthermore, it must engage in this self-questioning endlessly as the admission of complicity and the responsibility which that entails. Innocence clothes reading in the moment when reading comes to a halt. The guilty reading is not that reading which would strip bare its object. It is, on the contrary, that rhythmic event whereby reading is revealed, revealing itself, in its nakedness, and yet not totally so. Reading can never be completely naked, it can never be returned to a state of purity and innocence, back to some original act of innocent reading. For this would be to place ourselves – impossibly – before reading, before the movement of reading which is never done, and in which we find ourselves. Hence, the reading *we are guilty of*, the guilty reading which takes responsibility in shedding the illusion of an innocence.[6]

The scene of writing and of reading, is, like the grave, a private place. We must explore the contents of this privacy, in relation to what is publicly speakable, and draw the structure of confessions and denials of desire …
[…]
So. An image of a man. A typical man. A bourgeois man. Riven by guilt, silence and textuality. Forbidden to speak and yet incited to discourse, and therefore speaking in another place. Who says sing when he means fuck, who fears sex and calls it smallpox, who enjoys sex and calls it reading, who is fascinated and terrified by texts and so reads them once, but only for information's sake, who is sober and drunk. Who would rather burn his body, who would rather go blind, but who, as in the storm of rage with which he tears, elsewhere in the *Diary* his wife's pathetic love-letters, obliterates the texts instead.

A representation of a representation, moreover. Behind it all, not even an adulterous act, but an act of reading. A lewd book.

Francis Barker, *The Tremulous Private Body:*
Essays on Subjection (1984, 3–4, 9)

For some, however, there never could be the possibility of innocence, whether its illusion or otherwise. We are still caught up in guilt, through *an act of reading*. The book read: *L'escholle des filles*. The reader (that is, the textual figure whom Francis Barker reads), Samuel Pepys   *a representation of a representation, moreover*   the text in which Pepys confesses his guilt, in other words, privately to himself as the writer-confessor of the sinning reader: his diary, 9 February 1668.[7] (Indirectly, the text appears again in Pepys' diary, through his mention of seeing *The Country Wife*, in which the book is mentioned, and forbidden to be read.)

The passage read by Barker is not the only mention made by Pepys of this *lewd book* and it is instructive to consider the desire to read, which the possibility of reading guiltily engenders, and by which it is propelled. A detour, therefore, before considering Barker's passage. *L'escolle des filles ou La philosophie des dames, divisée en deux dialogues* (att. Michel Millot and Jean L'Ange (1655)), is first mentioned by Pepys on 13 January 1668[8]   *I was ashamed of reading it*   Pepys is not so ashamed of reading it, however, that, nearly a month later (8 February), he returns to the bookseller to purchase the book.[9] On the following day comes the passage with which Barker is concerned.[10] There is much that might be commented on between the three entries having to do with reading, had we the time. For now, however, we can only re-present the passages as annotated citations, deferring their reading (although that movement is ghosted here, indirectly), while guiltily alluding to the possibility of a future reading. Not least noteworthy are the matters of translation, return and reiteration, denial and avoidance, and the parenthetical statement, only partly legible in the manuscript, which climaxes in a kind of comic French, as though English were too proper a language, or otherwise improper, in which to record the response to reading.

Francis Barker addresses only the last of the three entries, omitting, furthermore, that partially unreadable, parenthetical overflow of the pen (see n. 4). What can be read in the first entry, from January, is the passing confession of another act of guilty reading, another *lewd book*, the *putanta errante*. Pepys gives his secret reading pleasures away, even as, through this allusion, he names that text, of which *L'escolle* is itself a reading. Not that Pepys acknowledges this directly, or that he has read the earlier Italian text. Also traceable across the three diary entries is the spacing and reiteration – the insistence with which Pepys acknowledges the text's *lewdness* is telling – which generates the very possibility of reading, as well as signing a desire to read, and to continue to do so. Thus, the passages articulate a representation of reading, a rhythm method building to a climax. Reading is itself the private, secret act, and the private record of the diary returns this event to its writer who reads himself coming back, so to speak, within a narrative of his own making, as simultaneously, subsumed by, and seeking to control, what it means to read.

Barker understands this. His first statement above expresses the over-flow within reading, more than reading itself, the movement whereby a reading is always traced by a writing. This double gesture is a figure of representation as re-presentation moreover. Reading re-presents what is not present, the other text, and, in this, Barker's text is no exception, re-presenting that representation of a reading, the text of which is neither simply there, nor not there. For the act of reading, in being a double move-ment of simulation and dissimulation, concerns itself with the impossi-bility of presentation, even though it is always concerned with what comes between representation and re-presentation. Reading thus opens that spacing, reading as spacing itself, in the suture of the hyphen of 're-presentation', and between the desire for *representation* and *re-presentation*.

And this is precisely what we are able to read in Francis Barker's text, wherein reading spaces and thereby performs in other words the articu-lation of Pepys' text of that already displaced *lewd book*. Barker's perform-ance opens reading as that which is always already remarked in an abyssal reduplication, whereby those two words, *lewd book*, read or, at least, desire to read Pepys' own diary, as much as they seek to return to us the con-dition of that which Pepys claims to read *for information's sake*. Indeed, in reading this, I do no more than enact the very condition of reading. Herein is the performative aspect of reiterative spacing, of deferral and displacement caught in a *representation of a representation* of a representation, and fuelled in this unveiling by the desire to read. This in turn is insepar-able from the analytical engagement.

Thus, while Pepys' diary is a spectacular revelation of the ways in which reading and writing mean to say one thing while saying quite another, or, perhaps, saying the one thing in quite another way, one tongue in the mouth of the other,[11] Barker's text reveals how the action of guilty reading – which phrase, 'guilty reading', is really to say nothing more than just *reading*, the salient quality of reading being that it is guilty[12] – can never escape its own complicity in the rhythm in question. Such reiterative process is caught everywhere, even as Barker confesses Pepys (who has already confessed himself), but nowhere more so, perhaps, than in that single word – *Riven*. Defining all the readings, and being a reading itself which says everything and nothing, this term perpetuates the division of the private scene. This works itself out in the subsequent sentence of Barker's text. Notice the insistent reiteration of that *who*, which seeks to pin down the subject, while serving, paradoxically, to trace the desire to read in the very rhythm of reading which those *who*s re-present, without representation.

Despite the obvious attempt to make plain what Pepys' reading is charged with obscuring, displacing, denying, Barker's own reading, in all its clausal divisions, disperses itself in its very performance. This gesture comes, again and again, despite that desire to reveal all, to give names, through the act of reading, to those acts which are themselves not acts but are, instead, revealed as *naming-readings*. Such a process, of what we might describe as a nominal-analytic, imposes a reading as a halt to reading, as though everything were said, and done with. Nothing other than an attempted act of mastery, Barker's text presents a moment of violent policing dressed up in the guise of re-presenting that which reading supposedly cannot say, even though the text succeeds only in representing reading, and that, moreover, as a movement, in which it is caught.

If, as Peter de Bolla suggests, reading is a process whereby the self identifies and thus attempts to stay the interpretation of the self,   *what is its difficulty such that it does not simply frustrate us but instead incites us, regardless of our desire for simplicity*   through a number of claims concerning itself,[13] then Francis Barker's text, in addressing the guilt of Pepys' secret act of reading so forcefully, reveals not only an act of reading, but also a reader. Or, perhaps, two readers, at least. For there is the reader Barker would appear to wish to be. Here is the reader who no longer has to read, who has everything under control. Furthermore, there is the reader who does not read either, but who awaits the arrival of the reading from some other place, as though everything that could be said, had been said, as though reading were over, and the text had said it all.

Why is the writerly our value? Because the goal of the literary work (of literature as work) is to make the reader no longer a consumer, but a producer of the text. Our literature is characterized by the pitiless divorce which the literary institution maintains between the producer of the text and its user, between its owner and its customer, between its author and its reader. This reader is thereby plunged into a kind of idleness – he is intransitive; he is, in short, *serious*: instead of functioning himself, instead of gaining access to the magic of the signifier, to the pleasure of writing, he is left with no more than the poor freedom either to accept or reject the text: reading is nothing more than a *referendum*. Opposite the writerly text, then, is its countervalue, its negative, reactive value: what can be read, but not written: the *readerly*. We call any readerly text a classic text.

Roland Barthes, *S/Z* (1974, 4)

Not reading as such, apparently, never this. Instead, the reader, idle, intransitive, suffering passively, to paraphrase Derrida, the violent imposition of the mark of writing, becoming the remark of reading. All of which might well be taken to be a commentary — a reading — in some fashion on the fragment taken from the text of Francis Barker, as a text belonging to the *literary institution*: the critic *malgré lui-même*. If *reading is nothing more than a referendum*, if it is reduced to nothing other than a process or principle of gathering the signifiers or referents so as to make a political decision, then reading is halted before it can begin. There can be no interest in reading, only in the action of connecting those traces which can be assigned a meaning or value in common, those which carry, bear, or carry back the same. The *fainéant* reader is allowed to seek for nothing other than this return for his or her effort, which is not really an effort at all, according to Barthes. There is only the choice to accept or not to accept.

And the readerly. That for which there can be no counter-signature of the critic or reader. That which, impassive and impressive, monumental even, is read as appearing to us as the always-already-having-been-read, ahead of reading, even in the event, anticipated by the author's act of writing. Is this possible, imaginable even? Barthes imagines it, imagining the impossible: that text which, no longer a text — if it ever was one — was always a book, a work, closed, finished, complete. Unified. Barthes's gesture is one which eviscerates, even as it delineates, naming literature as that which succumbs to division and disenfranchisement, wherein which process the reader is left nothing to do. Reading-as-referendum leaves nothing to be done.

This is, of course, a reading. My reading of Barthes's reading. Moreover, it is Barthes's reading of a situation. The reader, appalled by the solidity of the work, announces it as unreadable precisely because it is identified as the *readerly*, precisely because it is a text solidified into a work, which is read as delimiting ahead of the encounter with the reader all traces, all aporia, all play within the text or, more importantly, between the one and the other, between the work and the reader. The very idea. The reader, in this case Roland Barthes, in determining the nature or the condition of the book, a certain kind of book named literature, reading it as readerly, reads the impossibility of its being read by a reader. Other than himself. He reads its very unreadability and thereby suggests the impossibility of any other reader, other, that is, than himself. Having read it, having read what he claims is its readerly prohibition of readerly activity outside itself, Barthes effectively, like the character from a Kafka parable, prohibits entrance on the grounds that prohibition or movement is installed already.

But of course, Barthes acknowledges this paradox — to an extent, up to a certain point only. For Barthes concludes with the suggestion that that which is read as readerly is that which can only be read and not written. This gesture tyrannises with the effect of supposition: *as though*. It is *as though* or *as if* there could only ever be one kind of reading, the reading dictated by the text, and not the reading activated by the reader. (Notice that reading and writing remain two terms on either side of the structuralist divide, marked by a *pitiless divorce*.) Poor freedom indeed, a poor freedom replicated by Barthes in the movement of this passage, where the poor reader, impressed by that magisterial 'we' – *we call any readerly text a classic text* – can only choose to accept or reject the Barthesian proposition, the reading which closes the book on reading, dressed up as a referendum on reading, even as the proposition is put that this is (a reading of) reading which is *nothing more than a* referendum. Take it or leave it.

This is what, as readers, we are asked to do: to take it or leave it   *to accept or reject the text*   to vote on the proposal without reading it. Accepting, acquiescing, we are forced into idleness. Reading idles, it runs, ticking over, getting nowhere.

Of course, even in ticking over, there is no real standing still, there is, on the contrary, an undeniable oscillation which denies absolute stasis. Barthes's reading of idling and idleness, of the *pitiless divorce* between producer and user, owner and consumer, author and reader, readerly and writerly, is, in its performance of the law of literature and the scene of referendum, an ironic, witty *referent* to reading as referendum. In being this referent, it marks itself with that carrying back, that return that the referent names, inscribed in the very idea of the referendum, re-marking that return with a difference.

How do we read this? In the act of Barthes's risk of the reading, which performs the very gesture it would seek to resist. If Barthes asks us to activate the writerly or scriptible text, it is in order to mobilise reading as the production and not the consumption of the text. This much is clear. That this appears to be traced in and through what amounts to a classic structuralist serialisation of pairings and oppositions, ascending to some scientific apogee in the readerly/writerly distinction, is less clear, and all the more dangerous for all that. For the risk is taken in the act of Barthes's reading-as-imitation, as he teases out indirectly, as the condition of his reading, the ideological relations which enact the totalising certainty of a certain kind of reading.[14] He does so moreover, not through any clearly oppositional polemic, although his argument may be read as a polemic in one sense, in that it appears to position itself deliberately against the cultural construction of the readerly text. Yet the paradox, as we have shown, is that he does so, not in oppositional language but in the language of the literary institution.

So, to return to an earlier point: what Barthes's ironic performance suggests is that such a reading is not in fact one at all. It is an act of violent inscription on the reader, to which the reader can only respond through another binarism, acceptance or rejection, placing the X in the box on the referendum ballot paper, effectively erasing the self in abandoning the act of reading and, with that, the responsibility which all reading entails. At the same time, however, or nearly the same time – for there is still that question of timing, the oscillation which allows us to define the movement within idling, and thereby to define idling itself – even as Barthes reiterates the readerly in his reading, so he reads into the readerly a difference in the economy of the self-same, the passage playing out the tyranny of the readerly and the displacement from within which reading as production rather than as consumption makes possible. In this, Barthes operates a reading from within. This reading opens to us, and allows us to open, the 'theoretical' or the 'political' in those very places where such acts of reading have been discounted, unless of course such readings can be made to assume the identity of the referendum once again.

Post-theory has often become a thinly made-up return to pre-theoretical habits and a sort of intellectual journalism ...

[...]

'Theory', from this perspective, is (was) not political, or at any rate not political *enough*, never political enough, so it must be politicised. Politicising it means culturalising it ... culturalising it means historicising it, historicising it means interring it. The logic of this position ... going something like this: theory shows us that texts have no intrinsic identity in themselves independent of the readings they are given; reading is therefore essentially *free* with respect to the text being read; so the readings we in fact come up with must have motivations that are not prescribed by the text being read; those motivations are, like it or not, essentially political; so it is incumbent upon us, on the Left, to read for socialism, towards socialism. All *other* readings and reading methods are also therefore accountable in political terms, and most importantly, readings or reading methods that do not recognise this intrinsic politics of reading are *ipso facto* reactionary.

The ('theoretical') problem with this argument ... is that it is caught in a contradiction between the sense that meaning is indeterminate ... and a sense that it is determinable ... Knowing what we want (socialism) means being confident that we know what we mean – but this means that we believe *we* can write our texts – our readings – which are determinate with respect to their meanings, whereas our basic premise is that texts are radically indeterminate with respect to their meanings.

Geoffrey Bennington, '*Inter*' (1999, 106)

If we are to talk of 'theory' or 'politics', we have to acknowledge that, on the one hand, certain acts of close reading can be read as 'too theoretical' or 'too political'. On the other hand, those same readings, or different readings of a similar kind, can be read as 'not theoretical' or 'not political enough'. Often, it is a political decision to decide on the status of 'theory' and the kind of reading which 'it' supposedly produces. It is nothing other than a political reading, which often amounts to the same thing as a *strong* reading, which is not really a reading in the event, but, rather, the return of the referendum. From 1970 to 1999, then, and, all the while, between those dates, little seems to have changed. If there is a change, it is perhaps a changing of the guard. The *literary institution* remains exactly that, though what has become institutionalised, and what perhaps no longer reads because of the domestication effected through institutionalisation, is a politics (of reading), which wants to (not) read 'theory', but to present a 'reading' of the strong variety, and so have done with the very kind of activity which Barthes had imagined would be a necessary counter-signature to the enforced passivity sanctioned by the institution, in the name of literature.

What is the name of the prohibition of reading from the other side? In one sense, it has to be given the name of *post-theory*, as Geoffrey Bennington has defined that. *Post-theory*, having done with theory, having had enough to do with theory, having claimed to have read quite enough of what it misreads as 'theory' – in naming it 'theory', in providing an identity which can be described as an 'it' in the first place – decides that 'theory' was not, never was or is (or by the imposing temporal logic of such an argument, *never will be*), *political enough*. What is *political enough* for those who claim that this is not what 'theory' is, was, or shall be, is hardly ever read. The *political enough* remains within the realm of the unthought, except, of course, along institutional lines, which is another way of saying, from a certain perspective, the unread. The *political enough* is precisely what those who have read 'theory' as not *political enough* claim to be, though to what extent those who are *political enough* have read carefully what it means to be *political enough* remains unclear. Except that, in the name of no longer reading, those who are *political enough* can always justify their having done with reading, and specifically reading 'theory', exactly because they can say that they and their readings, so-called, are *political enough*.[15]

Bennington's analysis provides a clear enough assessment of the accusations levelled at certain kinds of reading   *there is no such thing as an innocent reading*   we are still with the guilty reading, therefore. However, what is also clear is that, on the side of (a) politics, not/reading allows for judgements to be made, guilt assigned. Since 1968 (let's say), the movement away from reading on the part of some has been accompanied by the inevitable evasion of the acknowledgement of complicity, which would make the continuance of reading undeniable. Also elided therefore must be the question *what is it to read?* With the act of sentencing – *not political enough, never political enough* – comes the pronouncement which has replaced that question: *we know what it means to read.* In a sense, there is a negative performative at work within this statement, which whispers *neither do we have to continue reading, nor do we have to read how others read, if this means reading differently.*

As Bennington points out, with guilt comes the death sentence and subsequent burial, which is nothing other than the inevitable outcome of the arrest of reading. *Politicising: culturalising: historicising: interring.* Bennington's reading reveals the extent to which the reading which is politicised within narrow ideological or institutional parameters expresses an attempted mastery over theory, even if this means rejecting it out of hand. With this sought-after mastery, there is expressed a desire to account for that which it addresses, whether the meaning of its own texts, or the texts of others, as part of a teleological process, where reading, in a totalising, utopian translation, means *reading-towards-socialism.*

However, in the face of this movement, Bennington offers a reading in the place of not-reading, which appears in the guise of *reading-towards-socialism.* Unfolding the logic and movement of the latter, his reading acts as a counter-signature to the seemingly inexorable progress. This gesture, tracing first the advance, and then, in turn, stalling it through the activity of a reading which proceeds as the necessary contrapuntal effect from within the place of the non-read of *reading-towards-socialism*, performs the urgent reason for the pursuit of reading. This reading performance on Bennington's part is itself the expression of the – political? – responsibility which every patient reading entails, and which it also addresses in the face of haste or an apparent reading process which is in fact the abandonment of reading in name of the project. Contrary to the project, in this case *socialism*, which would have done with reading, reading becomes all the more obligatory, all the more compelling, as that which still remains to come, if the reader is not to fall into the place of non-reading.

What does *reading-towards-socialism* fail to read? It fails, and in so doing abandons the pressing responsibility, to acknowledge the incommensurable aporia within its own logic, which Bennington's reading of reading brings into focus so tellingly, and which the passage we have cited performs with that ironic proximity necessary in all close reading. In producing a paraphrase of the politicised reading of theory's reading, it is shown at what point the politicised reading arrives at an *impasse.* Politicised reading maintains the precarious balancing trick of 'on the one hand, on the other', which is its theoretical problematic, and is that which installs the aporetic *between* the desire for determinate meaning and *the sense that meaning is indeterminate*. Yet, if we can begin to read the aporetic in *reading-towards-socialism* as a dual project which desires arrival and abandons reading as not being political enough, we may, perhaps, begin to understand, that is to say *read*, that the aporetic marks that place where responsibility begins. The aporia does not excuse us from responsibility;[16] it is, rather, responsibility itself, the responsibility to re-formulate the question of politics in the face of the limit of *reading-towards-socialism*, which, in seeking to make *All **other** readings and reading methods ... accountable in political terms*, cannot account for itself, and is, itself, found guilty of that of which it would seek to indict others. Reading, in one sense is always this: the response to the other as responsibility. Bennington's text manifests this responsibility through an act of reading which opens, rather than forecloses, on reading. In doing so, he makes it possible for others to read how political and institutional structures must be opened to a certain reading act, which extends beyond discourses or semantics, although these also remain to be read.[17]

'What is to be done?' must acknowledge the force of writing, its meta-phoricity and its rhetorical discourse, as a productive matrix which defines the 'social' and makes it available as an objective of[,] and for, action. Textuality is not simply a second-order ideological expression or a verbal symptom of a pre-given political subject. That the political subject ... is a discursive event is nowhere more clearly seen than in ... Mill's essay 'On Liberty' ... Rereading Mill through the strategies of 'writing' that I have suggested reveals that one cannot passively follow the line of argument running through the logic of the opposing ideology. The textual process of political antagonism initiates a contradictory process of reading between the lines; the agent of the discourse becomes, in the same time of utter-ance, the inverted, projected object of the argument, turned against itself. ... Reading Mill, against the grain, suggests that politics can only become representative, a truly public discourse, through a splitting in the signifi-cation of the subject of representation; through an ambivalence at the point of the enunciation of a politics.

[...]

   A critical discourse does not yield a *new* political object, or aim, or knowledge, which is simply a mimetic reflection of an a priori political principle or theoretical commitment. We should not demand of it a pure teleology of analysis whereby the prior principle is simply augmented, its rationality smoothly developed, its identity as socialist or materialist ... consistently confirmed in each oppositional stage of the argument. ... the language of critique is effective ... to the extent to which it overcomes the given grounds of opposition and opens up a space of translation: a place of hybridity ...

[...]

The progressive reading is crucially determined by the adversarial or agonistic situation itself; it is effective because it uses the subversive messy mask of camouflage and does not come like a pure avenging angel speak-ing the truth of a radical historicity and pure oppositionality.

Homi K. Bhabha, 'The Commitment to Theory'

(1994, 23–4, 25, 26)

What is to be done?

As an adjunct to the instituting question   *what is it to read?*   this new demand appears to make more insistent the question of reading differently. Moreover, the question is never one, even though readings must negotiate between singularity, exemplarity, and iterability. There is, therefore, not one question, not one reading. There are *questions*, and there are *readings*. Changing the formulation of the verb a little, why not state that *there must be readings*? And not simply many readings by different readers, as though I were advocating some form of academic or liberal pluralism (which I am not, nor could I, after Bennington);[18] instead, a series of readings by the same reader (who, it must be admitted can never be the same reader), which, in part, will serve to resist the idea of idleness imposed on the reader, as suggested by Barthes, while engaging in a *productive matrix* which, as an act of return and reiteration implicated in reading, *reveals that one cannot passively follow the line of argument*, whether that line is either, on the one hand, the logical progression, or, on the other, the party line of the ideological drive. To take this further, why not suggest, as does Bhabha, the necessity of hybridity and translation opened by the reading gesture? Whereby readings are installed and spaced within the act of reading's temporality, if reading is not merely to assume the teleological manifestation of the *reading-towards-socialism*, for example.

Indeed, and to take a single example, from the very arena of a radical politics, so-called, the very nature of the question   *what is to be done?*   demands that its reading can only ever be decided in the event of its articulation as a response to a situation. If this question offers to begin to read each situation *qua* political, equally, it demands that we read it as a different institution of reading with every articulation. Spaced by difference from itself, the question issues its demands at the semantic, discursive, political, and institutional levels simultaneously. It does so in more directions than one, the possibility of reading altering every time, and proliferating the possibility of future readings as the reformulated expression   *The textual process of political antagonism*   which, in turn inscribes the question as the referent, the carrying back, of reading itself, as that which makes a politics possible

reading between the lines

this is no doubt *messy*, to borrow Bhabha's word. Simplistically read, it appears to install – from a certain political position – the possibility of contradiction. If the question (of politics) is not the same, all the time, every time, the question of what is to be done is opened up from within, to the possibility of its own difference; it is – it reads itself, never quite as itself – as messy, hybrid, always already translated. This is its promise, and this is what we can read. The question becomes one of strategic speaking against the self, against the possibility of a pure undifferentiated self, which speech, which *reading*, is installed in the term *contradiction*. Speaking against the self, as the gesture *determined by the adversarial or agonistic situation*, always allows for reading to take on the mask. Assuming the guise of a performative authenticity, reading disables internally, from within the articulation of, on the one hand, the authoritative discourse, and on the other, some supposedly *pure oppositionality*. Reading thus makes possible what Bhabha describes as a *splitting in the signification of the subject of representation*.

Reading as undifferentiated augmentation or supplement to the truth of political discourse is never reading. It is, instead, passive reception and the promise of an equally passive future transmission where, in such an act of indifference, reading stops and something is lost in translation: the political itself, we might well suggest, in favour of the narrowly Political, the party line. Reading as contradiction is defined variously by Bhabha as reading between the lines,   *one must be able to stay nimble as one reflects, and stay on the 'surface' whilst reading between the lines*   reading against the grain, progressive reading. Reading as strategic mask, that which makes possible a *truly public discourse*, makes available reading itself, through the event of that torque on which all acts of reading are inevitably predicated. There can be no reading without the chance of the object being turned against itself, from within itself as the alterity of the subject opens the subject to the question, that is to say, to reading. The very idea of reading answers the question,   *what is to be done?*   even though it does not propose an answer as *the answer*, or even that there is such a thing as a single answer. What our understanding of reading makes possible is the answer as the promise of reading, in which can be heard the words of John Stuart Mill's text, to which Bhabha is in part responding   *it still remains to speak*   as a means of coming to terms with a commitment to theory.[19]

Those phrases of Bhabha's which punctuate the passage and which address the condition of reading are of interest: *reading between the lines, Reading … against the grain, The progressive reading.* None of these can be read as naming a reading programme (such as that defined by Bennington). Nor can they be transformed into a programme, a method, or template for a procedure. Throwing a spanner in the works of the narrowly political reading, they disable any possibility of a technics of reading (which would not be reading at all, as we have argued). However, they do suggest a reading activity, which is only similar to itself in being reading, and yet which is different in each event, and which is marked as different not only from other readings, but also as the difference (of reading) from within the apparent unity of the discursive object. Each phrase appears commonplace enough. So much so, in fact, that we might be tempted to take them for granted, not reading their significance as expressions of that *mask of camouflage*. In naming a movement of reading which resists a unity of definition or the *pure teleology of analysis*, such phrases are *camouflage* or *mask* without the suggestion of anything beneath or beyond. Thus in the very act of reading itself, reading swerves away from the implication that there is a final meaning that can be read, beyond reading and to which reading is subservient. Reading denies the end of reading, that we can have done with reading.

If to imagine is to misinterpret, which makes all poems antithetical to their precursors, then to imagine after a poet is to learn his own metaphors for his acts of reading. Criticism then necessarily becomes antithetical also, a series of swerves after unique acts of creative misunderstanding.

The first swerve is to learn to read a great precursor poet as his greater descendants compelled themselves to read him.

The second is to read the descendants as if we were their disciples, and so compel ourselves to learn where we must revise if we are to be found by our own work, and claimed by the living of our own lives.

Neither of these quests is yet Antithetical Criticism. That begins when we measure the first *clinamen* against the second. Finding just what the accent of deviation is, we proceed to apply it as corrective to the reading of the first but not the second poet or group of poets. To practice Antithetical Criticism on the more recent poet or poets becomes possible only when they have found disciples not ourselves. But these can be critics, and not poets.

It can be objected against this theory that we never read a poet as poet, but only read one poet in another poet, or even into another poet. Our answer is manifold: we deny that there is, was or ever can be a poet as poet – to a reader. Just as we can never embrace … a single person, but embrace the whole of her or his family romance, so we can never read a poet without reading the whole of his or her family romance as poet. The issue is reduction and how best to avoid it.

[...]

Every poem is a misinterpretation of a parent poem. A poem is not an overcoming of anxiety, but is that anxiety. Poets' misinterpretations or poems are more drastic than critics' misinterpretations or criticism, but this is only a difference in degree and not at all in kind. There are no interpretations but only misinterpretations, and so all criticism is prose poetry.

[...]

Every deep reader is an Idiot Questioner. He asks, 'who wrote my poem?'
                    Harold Bloom, *The Anxiety of Influence* (1973, 93–5, 96)

Reading continues, therefore. Never the same, reading swerves. It deviates from itself and within itself. This is not simply a dialectical or oppositional movement. It is, rather, the necessary and inevitable movement by which reading proceeds, even if reading becomes, or is always, misreading. (Which, in itself, as misinterpretation, is the imaginative swerve of the critical imagination.) This is the mark of difference which makes possible the rhythm of reading, whereby it becomes the inscription of a counter-signature to another text, a translation, in that oscillation between a reading and a writing. This is the case, even if there is that necessary sense of identification between the reader and what is read.[20] Indeed, that deviation of the counter-signature, the act of close reading which projects the alterity of the text being read, is itself unavoidably traced – even as it haunts or traces – the question of identification.

Reading always takes time.[21] It proceeds across time, as a matter of multiple temporalities: those of the reader and the narrator, for example. Furthermore, reading takes place, continues to take place, across time. From one reader to another, from one poet to another. At the same time, this suggests, as is well known, that reading remains, there is reading to-come.

The time of reading as misreading, misinterpretation, is Harold Bloom's concern. Bloom's seemingly dialectical imagination conceives criticism as an act of close reading not in absolute conformity to the text being read, the parent text. Rather it imagines – as its reading, in enacting the reading it desires as the future of reading-as-criticism – an antagonistic, as well as an agonistic performance in the movement of reading. As a result of anxiety, criticism, critical reading, can come to inhabit, in and through misreading, a poetic space, that is to say a space which opens through misreading and which is thus a poetic event. This at least is (my reading of) Bloom's reading of the imagined reading, an imaginary of reading as misreading or misinterpretation. Misprision is figured as the swerve away from, on the one hand, the slavish faithfulness   *the prior principle is simply augmented*   of impoverished paraphrase   *a mimetic reflection*   and, on the other hand, the partiality of that which claims to be a reading in the name of some programme or method. Reading must swerve to avoid reduction. It must swerve to evade its own act of reduction, a double apophanic movement which, in reducing the other text, reduces itself also, to the outline, the parody of reading. This is, in one instance, one possible reading of reading in the Bloomian imaginary.

The question of reading as avoidance is not, of course, avoidance at all, unless it be the avoidance of avoidance which more partial, less anxious 'readings', so-called, manifest in their critical acts. The avoidance of avoid-ance is an engagement, a return to reading, a return via reading to the intimacy of reading's misinterpretation, as Bloom puts it. Thus, Bloom situates reading, in the name of reading, against so-called reading, which gestures are really for Bloom formal devices for the reductive containment of the paternal text. However, Antithetical Criticism, that critical mis-understanding which Bloom desires as the read figure of the place which reading should inhabit, is the properly Oedipal struggle that never escapes that which it seeks to overthrow, and only succeeds in embedding within itself the traces of its precursors (which are always already there though not yet read).

However, this embedding, or sedimentation of the trace, is perhaps readable or misreadable as the reading itself and not the embedding, even though it is arguably misread as that. For sedimentation has always already taken place. What takes place subsequently is the reading as event. The act of reading is thus comprehended as the interpretive gesture of some apparently discerned a priori sedimentation, where the trace is read and thereby made to surface amongst a host of other signals, yet which is not the prior text as such, only that read as that which is left behind, that which makes reading possible in the first place, as the negotiation between absences.

An unresolvable tension between the assumption — which is to say the reading, after a fashion — of particular constructions of position remains. Such tension allows (the) future (of) reading to be imagined. But the reading Bloom imagines not only takes place as the critical event, as he makes explicit. It seeks to take the place of the poet who reads, even though it knows this can never be completed. Hence the desire to read, and the need to continue reading in the face of the unresolvable tension, which opens rather than closes the act, turning it away from itself. All poetic texts are signed indelibly by the act of reading. This is inescapable, and we must learn how to read to what extent reading is a radical mis-interpretation. Critical reading must learn how to read in this manner, learning to read by reading that *accent of deviation* which has determined the writing of — and *reading* in — poetry by those who are indebted to the *precursor poet*. Reading this poet *as his greater descendants* read him is the first gesture in learning to (mis)read. Coming to terms with this, reading must then read those descendants in a similar manner as preparation for Antithetical Criticism.

This obligatory manœuvre articulates the responsibility of reading, already discussed in part elsewhere. If we ourselves wish to be read by those who come after, argues Bloom, our responsibility entails learning how to avoid the programme as the excuse for reading. Furthermore, our responsibility is to read, knowing all the while that we will only ever misread, and knowing also that that after which we read, time after time, and that which we name the poetic, is, if not ineffable exactly, then certainly, unreadable as such. For that after which we seek is from and of the other, so to speak.[22] Yet, the poetic avoids, swerving away from reading, keeping its secret to itself, while remaining in plain view, directing us ceaselessly into that act of misprision. Reading thus becomes caught in the impossible double bind. Seeking to abolish the distance between that on which it discourses and the manner of its act, it will never entirely take the place of that which it attempts to read, even though we take the time to read of that displacement. Hence, anxiety: hence, the desire to read. Hence, the impossible responsibility   *Everything we read:* *remains*   of asking all the while *who wrote my poem?*

Who wrote my poem? What is to be done? How to translate?

What is it to read?

Paris is Burning (1991) is a film ... about drag balls in New York City, attended by, performed by 'men' who are either African-American or Latino. The balls are contests in which the contestants compete under a variety of categories. ... 'Realness' is not exactly a category in which one competes; it is a standard that is used to judge any given performance within the established categories. And yet what determines the effect of realness is the ability to compel belief, to produce the naturalized effect. This effect is the result of an embodiment of norms, an impersonation of a racial and class norm, a norm which is at once a figure, a figure of a body, which is no particular body, but a morphological ideal that remains the standard which regulates the performance, but which no performance fully approximates.

Significantly, this is a performance that works, that effects realness, to the extent that it *cannot* be read. For 'reading' means taking someone down, exposing what fails to work at the level of appearance ... For a performance to work, then, means that a reading is no longer possible, or that a reading, an interpretation, appears to be a kind of transparent seeing, where what appears and what it means coincide. On the contrary, when what appears and how it is 'read' diverge, the artifice of perform-ance can be read as artifice; the ideal splits off from its appropriation. But the impossibility of reading means that the artifice works, the approxi-mation of realness appears to be achieved, the body performing and the ideal performed appear indistinguishable.

Judith Butler, *Bodies that Matter: On the Discursive Limits of 'Sex'* (1993, 128–9)

Of course, to paraphrase and twist Nicholas Royle just a little, there is reading and then there is reading, even if one, or the other, is, if not *not* reading, then the failure of reading, or, from the other side, the resistance to reading.[23] It is this that concerns Judith Butler in her concern for questions of performativity and reading.

The concern over what can be read, and that which resists reading of a particular kind, involves a commentary on a filmed performance   *a representation of a representation … an act of reading*   the performances in question being New York drag balls. The standard of performance is judged by the performer's ability to project the performance not as itself but as 'realness'. That is to say, as Butler suggests, that the performance is effected to such a degree, that in the act of performance, all performativity appears to give way to the irreality of a *morphological ideal*. This is Butler's reading, and it is a reading which is itself constructed through the reading which the film *Paris is Burning* constructs and performs. There is in the interpretation of the drag performance the assumption of failure and limit, of course, for no performance can fully approximate the *realness* it emulates and simulates. However *real* the performance, we are always aware that we are in the presence of an act.

Nevertheless, *realness*, in the sense interpreted by Butler, is that which, in being a successful performative act, **cannot** be read. The performance is thus split; it goes in two directions at once. There is that aspect of the act which is its performative authenticity, while there is also its enunciation of the limit to which artifice can go, which, we are tempted to suggest, is the limit also of reading. This is a double limit, even as there is a bifurcation, an opening in the act reliant on divergence, despite the standard of the real to which performance aspires, and which the performing body desires. Reading, according to Butler, can no longer read this performance, which is itself a self-conscious act of reading the ideal subject, unless it can read it as artifice, which is to say that reading fails precisely because it reaches a limit at which the artifice − the reading of *realness* − returns its own reading in the face of reading's apparent failure. In this, the drag per-formance is an act of impossible citation, a performance moreover of affirmative resistance. Resisting reading, that reading which would insist that the performance is, after all, only a performance, and therefore not authentic, the moment of the performative affirms itself as the only read-ing available. That reading of the subject which constitutes performance and, in doing so, elides the performative, sliding it under the real, dis-mantles reading's ability to speak of that which is inauthentic, that which, in the eyes of the reader, belongs to the order of the simulacrum rather than the real.

The apparent paradox in which we are enmeshed − we read that we can no longer read, because the work of reading is halted by an act of reading in the guise of the performance – brings back all those troublesome questions: *How to translate? What is to be done? What is it to read?* Butler's struggle with the question of reading's impossibility in the face of performative *realness* brings them back with a force. There is a sense that the reader is confronted, once more, by the readerly text in the form of drag, where, because all the questions are forestalled in the performance, even as they return, the reader is left as the passive observer   *plunged into a kind of idleness*   there is, however, another way around this impasse, and the passivity into which the readerly *realness* delivers the reader.

For Butler, reading suggests the possibility of exposing failure, those places where the text, in this case the costume, mannerisms, posture or gestures, make-up, delivery, of the drag artist, does not achieve the *naturalized effect*, and belief is established with that necessary degree of instantaneity. Yet, as I have proposed, the manifestation of the performer is, itself, an act of reading, of translation and interpretation, which takes time. This time taken, in determining what asserts realness and thus resists reading, is nothing other than the time of reading, of assembly and delineation, accretion and in-habitation. The signs of the body, of another's body, are assumed, taken on as habit, to the extent that the drag performance, which dictates interpretation only as *a kind of transparent seeing*, takes on that kind of verisimilitude and transparency associated conventionally with the nineteenth-century realist novel, or what Roland Barthes calls, above, *a classic text*.

Yet, with a difference.

For, here, in the drag performance, what becomes habituated, apparently domesticated and therefore beyond the possibility of reading, is the translation of the domestic, of transparency, into performance. With that comes the subversive presumption that any seemingly natural or naturalised representation can always be taken over, delegitimated in the act of apparently faithful reading, which performance seeks to be. Thus drag is, we would argue, a manifestation of that progressive reading spoken of by Homi Bhabha   *the subversive messy mask of camouflage*   in the event of performance, it is readable as the progressive reading itself. Seeking to install itself in the real, in the normative, it reads, and can be read as teaching us how to read, that the normative, the domestic, the conventional, and, moreover, the real, are constructs, acts or performances, and that we have only forgotten this to the extent that we no longer attempt to read them differently. We may not be able to 'read' the performance, but we can read its way of reading, reading its rhetoric differently. We can read that we cannot read, and, in this step, acknowledge the limits to which reading can go, while at the same time come to terms with what remains to be read, what propels us in our responsibility to continue reading.

'I've learned to tear up nothing of what I write,' Clarice Lispector tells me. But then comes the time for separation. The time for publication.

I would like so much this unknown untorn page. Everything we read: remains.

Hélène Cixous, 'Without end, no, State of drawingness, no, rather: The Executioner's taking off' (1998, 20)

It is becoming apparent that there is a matter of orientation with which we should concern ourselves. The situation of reading always dictates this. If nothing could have been read there would have been no commentary on reading and its difficulty in the face of performance. Judith Butler would not have been able to read the resistance to interpretation staged by the *realness* of certain drag performances. (Arguably, a certain, if limited, act of reading is taking place which allows for the distinction between reading and not reading, between those drag acts which are read as attaining *realness* and those which do not, and which, therefore, can be read.) So, there is, then, this issue of relationship, expressed in the suggestion that we read as philosophers, as opposed, let us say, to reading in a deterministic or technical fashion. There is also the question of how we situate ourselves in relation to a representation of a representation, to the private act, the public discourse, or to the readerly text. There is the matter of orientation in the face of a resistance to theory in the name of reading, a *reading-towards-socialism*, or the matter of learning how to read that accent of deviation which determines the reading of others. There is, furthermore, the situation of reading and its orientation to that which apparently prohibits or proscribes reading, yet which, nonetheless, situates itself as a reading between the lines or against the grain, whether what is being spoken of is political discourse or the drag performance. (I would argue that such a performance is readable as another political discourse, which, as different as it may seem, still can be read as coming down to questions of how to read the constitution of the subject, as does the text of John Stuart Mill, albeit in a highly different manner.) All of which leaves us with the secret and the confession.

Everything we read: remains.

This statement simultaneously keeps its secrets and reveals them, placing them in plain view, in the light of day. Do we know how to read this? Can we begin to orient ourselves? *Where to begin?* This performative sentence disorganises ahead, and in the event, of reading's efforts all reading, simply considered. It disjoints the time of reading as any simple time. Giving everything away at once, the words of Hélène Cixous speak of attempted readings in the past and the very idea of readings to come. There is no essential unity to this remark. In its disunity the statement is a reading – perhaps even the most *real* of performances, commentary in the guise of reading – of all acts of reading properly considered, at once the most obvious and (because of that) the most repeatedly forgotten, concerning the nature of reading. In forgetting the condition, the dis–orientation of which Cixous writes, readers seek to raise, explicitly or implicitly, acts of reading to the level of a generality.

What disorganises here? What installs the disunity into the sentence and, therefore, its reading? A very little thing, indeed. Almost nothing. Silent. Inarticulate. The mute sign of a certain passage, a processing, disarticulating the time of reading in the event of reading. The colon, that which is, at one and the same time, the greater part of the large intestine, the guts, otherwise the *reads*, and the punctuating pause of intermediate length, marking a distinct break in either a sentence or a rhythmical period. More commonly, it is that punctuation which signs the discontinuity of grammatical construction, usually, though not always, indicating antithesis, illustration, quotation, or listing.

This disturbance in continuity and rhythm serves to direct our reading both backwards and forwards, even while what remains towards, as, the end of the sentence – *remains* – might be read as that which is antithetical, illustrative, or the citation of the clause with which the sentence begins. So:

Everything that remains is that which we have not read.
Everything that remains is that which we have not yet read.
Everything that remains is that which we have yet to read.
Remains are what there are after we have read.
Remains are what there are to be read.
What remains after we have read are the remains.
What remains to be read: everything.
Everything that remains is what we have read.

Remains thus names everything and nothing as such. It names that which we have left behind in our acts of reading, those remains of texts, for example, for which our readings have been unable to account, and which, therefore, remain as yet unread, and still to be read. The remains of reading remain. As such, they remain as the unread, past and future, at the same time, though not the same time at all, in the temporal disorganisation of reading.

Remains thus names the very undecidability which reading encounters, which close acts of reading open to the reader, and which, concomitantly, project the reader towards future readings, as, once again, the responsibility of reading, in the face of the undecidable: (of that which) *remains.* Through Cixous's formulation, we can learn to read this, even as we are put in the position of not knowing quite how to situate ourselves, how to orient our reading of this statement. What we can read, nevertheless is that Cixous's statement, enacting the condition of reading, inscribes the inescapable circumstance or predicament faced in *everything we read.* Everything remains.

Here is one possible reading, another, one of several. It says and does not say the same. It says it without saying it. Without the plural subject,

without the community of readers, this phrase, *everything remains*, addresses
what reading fails to grasp, what it leaves behind, what it does not read,
while, all the while, and as the remainder of the statement, it reminds us
that everything remains to be read. The impossible logic of this statement
only compounds, condenses, and yet opens out what is to be read in
Hélène Cixous's remark. There is no getting around or, for that matter,
beyond this. However we seek to read this sentence, we always come back
to reading.

   Might it be possible to stabilise the statement by recourse to its context?
There is that remark, a chance observation, made by Clarice Lispector, and
brought back in writing by Cixous, as the reported words of another. But
it is still a question of the remains, the remainder, what remains, and,
specifically, unread   *this unknown untorn page*   unknown, untorn,
unwritten, not yet written, not yet read, already written, but not yet read.
The untorn page, a rem(a)inder, of all that comes before the printed,
published word   *public discourse*   which Cixous so desires, and
yet, also, secret, hidden from view, neither there nor not there   *like the
grave, a private place*   but, then, of course

Not everyone carries out the act of reading in the same way, but there is a manner of reading comparable to the act of writing – it's an act that suppresses the world. We annihilate the world with a book. You take the book you have opened, either knowingly or unknowingly, but often with an intimation that this book may be an instrument of separation. As soon as you open the book as a door, you enter another world, you close the door on this world. Reading is escaping in broad daylight, it's the rejection of the other; most of the time it's a solitary act, exactly like writing. We don't always think of this because we no longer read; we used to read when we were children and knew how violent reading can be. The book strikes a blow, but you, with your book, strike the outside world with an equal blow. We cannot write in any other way – without slamming the door, without cutting the ties. ...

[...]

When I write I escape myself, I uproot myself, I am a virgin; I leave from within my own house and I don't return. The moment I pick up my pen – magical gesture – I forget all the people I love; an hour later they are not born and I have never known them. Yet we do return. But for the duration of the journey we are killers. (Not only when we write, when we read too. Writing and reading are not separate, reading is a part of writing. A real reader is a writer, A real reader is already on the way to writing.)

[...]

It's also a clandestine, furtive act. We don't acknowledge it. It confuses. Reading is not as insignificant as we claim. First we must steal the key to the library. Reading is a provocation, a rebellion: we open the book's door, pretending it is a simple paperback cover, and in broad daylight escape! We are no longer there: this is what real reading is. If we haven't left the room, if we haven't gone over the wall, we're not reading. If we're only making believe we're there, if we're pretending before the eyes of the family, then we're reading. We are eating. Reading is eating on the sly.

Reading is eating the forbidden fruit, making forbidden love, changing eras, changing families, changing destinies, and changing day for night. Reading is doing everything exactly as we want and 'on the sly.'

Hélène Cixous, *Three Steps on the Ladder of Writing* (1993, 19–22) *not everyone carries out the act of reading in the same way* even if the assumption has been, occasionally, that there is only one way to read, whether we are speaking of the practice of close reading, so-called, or what is called *reading-towards-socialism*, for example. Cixous is one of the most patient of readers, one of the most generous, untiring, and enquiring. She reads, and lovingly acknowledges reading with *that impulse of identification which is indispensable for reading.* She acknowledges also that guilt which is indissociable from reading, bringing her reader back, and bringing back to us, the private place of reading and writing   *a solitary act*   we read guiltily, and therein is its pleasure, that indescribable sensation which can only be obtained through escape, secrecy, and consumption. Reading consumes our worldly identities even as we consume (in) reading: the sensual reciprocity with the other, that pleasure which comes only in giving oneself up to the *clandestine, furtive act*, to all that is forbidden. The greatest pleasure is in doing it in secret, but right before everyone else, in plain view, *before the eyes of the family.* But still,   *not everyone carries out the act of reading in the same way*   which perhaps may explain in part the pleasure, without getting any closer to the secret. Every act of reading is singular, even – especially – the act of rereading. Reading names escape for Cixous, an escape which is simultaneously a movement into the word and out of the world. In this, reading is comparable to writing, and it is in this comparison that reading is defined here, even though not every act of reading is the same, and *not everyone carries out reading in the same way.* The act of reading imagined by Cixous   *If to imagine is to misinterpret, which makes all poems antithetical to their precursors, then to imagine after a poet is to learn his own metaphors for his acts of reading*   is traced in that ineluctable slippage, from a reading to a writing which marks all true reading. However, even as we acknowledge this to be the case, we still have to understand to what extent this provisional definition of reading which Cixous provides does not reduce reading to a uniform practice, a shared act that is the same for everyone or the same every time.

Thus there is read in this oscillation the difficult negotiation between singularity and generality. There is a transaction between what is singular in the act of reading and what is iterable. Paradoxically, the singularity of the text is made known through its transmissibility. The transition effected in reading/writing is, for Cixous, the passage out, into another world, while being also the escape into the forbidden library. (It is forbidden to the extent that the key *must* be stolen.) In being explained, such secretive, solitary passage nonetheless gives nothing away. It is this perhaps which confuses, as much as the significance of reading. Reading thus escapes, taking flight ahead of all attempted acts of reading, any single definition of what reading might or might not be. Its secret significance lies in the fact that *we don't acknowledge it*, even though, paradoxically again, it appears that reading is only accorded recognition as that which is insignificant. Yet, in assigning this insignificance to reading, a reading – which is also an evasion as well as an identity for reading which allows it to avoid definition – is imposed.

How then does Cixous name reading, without naming it? How does she identify the very situation which reading makes possible, which is itself, and which it gives access to for the reader, without pinning reading down to the act of reading carried out in the same way? What is the silent name which is readable between the lines as a possible figure for reading? *Hejira* – that departure from home, from family and friends. This departure transforms, translating the reading subject. It makes possible change and freedom   *doing everything exactly as we want*   if reading escapes, however, there is always that predicament for the reader that reading departs ahead of the act. The reader can never catch up, nowhere more so than in that very moment where reading slides into writing, into eating, into *forbidden love. Already on the way to writing*: this describes what it is to read, while accounting for the fact that we have not yet done with reading, and that we cannot keep up with its movement. This marks an encounter with the unreadable, that moment when, far from bringing reading to a crashing halt   *how violent reading can be*   the reader is faced with the compelling evidence that reading must continue. Reading can occur only at another moment, elsewhere, not here, not now, not for good. This is read by Cixous in that concession of what reading changes. Reading remains unreadable to that extent that reading must begin again.[24] Already on the way to reading, there is, in the negotiation of this passage between what can be said about reading and what is unreadable, the tacit articulation of the remark that has already escaped

Everything we read: remains

and which speaks of reading's escape

It is again a question of 'the other' ... this term names the event in poetry, meaning and inscription which escapes human control, grounding or anticipation ... The *other* is engaged in writing in terms of an ineluctable secondarity in written meaning – for even in being inscribed the written presents itself as simultaneously *read* through the resonance of significations unanticipated in the act of inscription ... The other names the space 'of deferred reciprocity between reading and writing'.

Timothy Clark, *Derrida, Heidegger, Blanchot: Sources of Derrida's Notion and Practice of Literature* (1992, 110–11)

If reading, in the final analysis, escapes, if the text evades absolute definition while providing a possible means of escape, there are occasions when a certain resemblance of reading, perhaps nothing more than an apparition, will return to haunt the scene of the crime.

There is a ghost here, at work.[25] The other, that which *presents itself as simultaneously* **read**, haunts Timothy Clark's words. This is, perhaps, a deliberate performative operation, an improper citation which comes and goes almost too quickly. It is a question of speed, the speed at which the other, the spectre, returns, and, in returning, retreats. The frequency of telecommunication interrupts the calm surface of the page. Words interrupt the expression of the other within the writing of the citation. A resonance is established which is irreducible. Clark's writing presents itself as simultaneously *read*, even as it seeks to read, and, in so doing, to write   *A real reader is already on the way to writing*   the figure of the other countersigns the act of writing. In this, the signature of the other, that inscription of the unanticipated event within whatever we seek to write as a reading, appears to read our text.

As 'the other' names that event, so *event* is a kind of naming. *Event* names not the place of the other, for this would be to assign, however implicitly, the aura of a static unity for the other, although this is only dimly apprehended. Instead, it should be understood that *event* names, not the place, to reiterate the point, but that which takes place.

What takes place in the event, as the taking place of the event which is named by Clark the other, is that act of *unanticipated* reading. Reading, as we have said, takes time, and *event* names the time of reading, even if such time, escaping human control, is not our time – not my time, not your time. The time of reading, that of the event of secondarity *and* simultaneity, is, thus, untimely, never quite at the same time (even as itself).

However, if the *event* which the other's reading marks is that of a temporal displacement within and against the act of writing, then the other is also comprehended as a spacing. The other at work in our writing, and which makes the writing possible, not only causes a dis-placement as that necessary temporal possibility of a writing, it also spaces writing and, in doing so, makes it available to another reading. Writing as a reading remains unfinished therefore. Displaced in its own movement and response to the other, writing begins to slide immediately into the place of secondarity, into the place of that which remains to be read.

This is readable to the extent that the passage remains unreadable, although it strives to read, in part, that other discussion of reading which, in being written about, comes back, presenting Clark's writing as, itself, *simultaneously* **read**. In this situation, Clark's writing/reading reveals the condition of every text. Always remaining to be read, the text is unreadable, inasmuch as it cannot be decisively determined.[26] As Clark's discussion of Derrida returns to Derrida, and as Derrida returns via Clark, so this act of following the movement of Clark's inscription *and* that counter-movement, the *back-and-forth* within Timothy Clark's text of Derrida's writing – which is also a reading concerning the difficulty of reading conclusively when seeking to negotiate with the other in writing – fails to read in its act the reiteration of those prior texts. Furthermore, this pursuance of textual doubling, in opening this movement, in 'opening' a movement which has already undergone a process of unfolding, tacitly acknowledges through the abyssal structure onto which it is entering that it will itself be subject to repetition, displaced through other writings, other readings   *reading has no end, but is always to-come as work of the other ... a text never comes to rest in a unity or meaning finally revealed*   as others have already suggested, elsewhere, and as the citation from the text of Timothy Clark both implies and performs.

Derrida's return ghosts through Clark's own prose. In a sporadic, attenuated fashion, his critical negotiation between reading and writing addresses us: *secondarity ... written meaning presents itself ... simultaneously* **read**. This is not a question of a general hauntedness in the passage, so much as the fact that, in the citation, Derrida's words rhythmically interrupt, while simultaneously dictating Clark's writing as the other's resonance. We are witness to the situation of force and signification that inscribes the written, disrupting the reading process, as *The **other** is engaged in writing in terms of an ineluctable secondarity within meaning   a representation of a representation*   the signification at work here is not that of one text's simple reference to another, to a prior text. Clark's passage is, in some sense, a paraphrase of and countersignature for Derrida's 'Force and Signification', though it does not escape its haunted condition. The emergence of the 'prior' text, re-citing itself and prescribing the writing comprises its own signification, at the expense of critical commentary, and enacting in an unanticipated fashion that *power of repetition in alterity*. The *affirmation and nonfulfilment* which entail all acts of reading are, and will continue to be, remarked here. And so too is that guilty acknowledgement of complicity which articulates the oscillation between every reading/writing.

The *clôtural* structure of textuality is indicated by the transgression and restoration of closure, where both the transgression and the restoration are maintained in a non-symmetrical and non-totalizable relation, a relation in which the *relata* remain absolute. This *clôtural* structure is provoked by an act of *reading* whereby two irreconcilable lines of thought open up within a text. The *clôtural* reading has two moments which, because they are produced only within a particular reading, vary according to the text that is being read. However, without wishing to reduce the specificity of *clôtural* reading, the following general pattern can be delineated. First, the text is engaged in a repetition of its internal exigencies through an act of 'commentary'. Second, within and through this repetition, an ellipsis, or moment of alterity, opens up within the text which allows it to deliver itself up to a wholly other reading. It is of vital importance to emphasize that the moment of alterity, the ellipsis within the text, is glimpsed only by giving oneself up to textual repetition. The ellipsis is the space within repetition.

Clôtural reading is in-*fin*-ite that is, without end, apocalypse, or *eschaton*. It is situated in relation to an epoch that is closed, whose conceptuality is suspended or exhausted, but whose duration is possibly infinite ... *Clôtural* reading is the interruption of this epoch, the infinite deferral of its enclosing power through the alternation of repetition and alterity ... The possibility of *clôtural* reading arises only in relation to a specific and completed historical configuration which it ceaselessly seeks to repeat and interrupt.

Simon Critchley, *The Ethics of Deconstruction:*
Derrida and Levinas (1992, 88–9)

If complete escape is impossible, it is still possible to consider the possibility to come, in or through some im/possible relation. To read schematically, and yet to move elsewhere. To transport reading, in the act of reading, beyond the merely schematic, or otherwise across that boundary established in a reading which seemingly halts in a gesture of closure or finality. To repeat, in order to give *oneself up to textual repetition* and yet, through that very rhythmic recurrence of repetition, that coda in which is traced the structure of a writing, to open within that form the space where reading projects itself as still to come, not as the possible moment of closure in the future, but as the unfulfillable promise of reading's futurity, and, with that, its structural openness.

The structure of Simon Critchley's text enacts that which has just been described. It engages in its own commentary as the performance of that delineation, so that it is, in the same place, at the same moment, double. It inscribes and describes. It moves beyond itself in mapping the spacing of reading it desires and which it seeks to schematise – if only so as to move beyond the *schema* or *schemata* – as that which is named the **clôtural** *reading*.

Critchley's text assumes the form of the patient commentary concerning a form of reading, which observes how a text is internally marked   *riven*   by a contradictory doubleness, named in this case *transgression* and *restoration*. Both figures speak of closure, the former as the illicit, the guilty, transition beyond closure, the latter, the reconstruction of closure. Both, according to Critchley, are capable of existence, expressed as a mutual relationship between the two figures, in which relationship, the figures are incommensurable with one another, and, in turn, remain closed to each other, assigned their own closure. (And yet, in some measure, do they not also transgress that closure, in bearing, however, asymmetrically, a relation to each other?) Importantly, the two figures cannot be subsumed by some greater structural relationship which would totalise and economise on the figures of *transgression* and *restoration*. At the same time, the figure of the figures in question, which might perhaps be described as a step beyond and a turn or return, is not marked by an equivalence.

What makes such a contradictory configuration available? Reading, that reading which, in observing the **clôtural** *structure* is, itself, written as a **clôtural** *reading*, and is, therefore, structured in turn by the **clôtural** *structure of textuality*, which, of course, is available to *an act of reading whereby two irreconcilable lines of thought open up within a text. Transgression* and *restoration*. In naming this structure, in reading it in effect, Critchley is simultaneously making his own textual explanation turn on itself, in order to move elsewhere, beyond the fact of faithful commentary. Elucidation causes expansion.

Significantly, those *two irreconcilable lines* are never the same in every act of reading, as Critchley makes clear. It is not possible, therefore, in reading the structure in question, to elevate either *transgression* or *restoration* to the level of general principles. Although we may be tempted to read these terms according to a conceptual generality, the fact remains that each instance of *transgression*, each instance of *restoration*, remains irreducibly singular, *according to the text being read*. Thus, in this double, contradictory inscription – *transgression **and** reformation* – there is traced the doubling of *two irreconcilable lines*. For, not only are the two terms mutually exclusive (as we have already proposed), being what Critchley defines as absolute *relata*, their operation in the ***clôtural** structure of* Critchley's text can be submitted to the kind of reading the critic proposes.

Thus we can read, in these two redoubling terms, at the same moment, a contrary operation. Each term appears to move towards, or is otherwise available to a reading of, conceptual generalisation, whereby a scheme for reading is named, if, on the one hand, we seek to inaugurate an act of *reading-for-transgression* (in the same manner every time), or, on the other hand, if our reading is a *reading-for-restoration* (again, in the same manner every time). However, and here is the irreducible contrariety, each term, even as it gestures towards its installation as a general concept of reading, names the structure of the text and the structure of the reading which *vary according to the text that is being read*

*It is therefore a special reading which exculpates itself as a reading by posing every guilty reading the very question that unmasks its innocence, the mere question of its innocence: **what is it to read***?

thus, the necessities of repetition, in which all acts of reading are engaged. Repetition is most obviously at work in the text in the guise of commentary. In saying this, we are not saying anything new. Indeed, Simon Critchley says as much in seeking to delineate the ***clôtural** reading* without reducing the *specificity* of the imagined act. Commentary as repetition is, then, the first step in the act of ***clôtural** reading*. Nevertheless, in reiterating this commentary – and it *is* a commentary, inasmuch as it describes the process in question, in that tricky negotiation between delineation and singular specificity – it must be observed that commentary can never be a first step, in being an act of repetition. All commentary is therefore caught in a *non-symmetrical and non-totalizable relation*.

***Clôtural** reading* moves beyond the 'first' step, which is, as we have just insisted, never simply a *first* step, never wholly an originating, primary movement. Its second step, as Critchley describes it, is the event of opening made possible by repetition. An *ellipsis, or moment of alterity, opens up within the text which allows it to deliver itself up to a wholly other reading*.

The availability of ellipsis or alterity is only possible through repetition, through the *space within repetition*. Reading thus takes place as the event made possible by the spacing of the other, the other's spacing within the self-same which repetition appears to enact. This space or *moment of alterity*, it might be suggested, is readable in that reading of the first step which can never be one. Acknowledging that there is never a first step which is not always already a movement of repetition, we read the irreducible interval which is installed within the critic's text.

Reading as it is imagined here is   *without end, apocalypse, or* **eschaton**   never-ending, it names a spatio-temporal act the *duration* of which cannot be *defined*. The principle of the act of reading denies the dream of or desire for a final event, a last reading which, as part of some divine plan, exhausts and ends all other readings. Opening itself to alterity, to that other within, by which chance all reading is imaginable, the act of reading acknowledges not only the impossibility of the end (of reading, for example), but of the impossibility of reading without the opening of the other, and opening to the other, as the responsibility of reading.

The resistance to theory is a resistance to the rhetorical or tropological dimension of language, a dimension which is perhaps more explicitly in the foreground in literature (broadly conceived) than in other verbal manifestations or – to be somewhat less vague – which can be revealed in any verbal event when it is read textually. Since grammar as well as figuration is an integral part of reading, it follows that reading will be a negative process in which the grammatical cognition is undone, at all times, by its rhetorical displacement.

Paul de Man, *The Resistance to Theory* (1986, 17)

Repetition names certain *rhetorical* or *tropological* structures, along with *figuration*, which remain singular while being readable as repetitious in condition. It is thus part of the very fabric of the text, one aspect of textuality itself. In repeating the structure of the text through reading, it is necessary to read that repetition, even as repetition becomes repeated in the attempt to read carefully and faithfully. It is very much a matter of reading *textually*, as Paul de Man puts it.

However, it is precisely in the face of reading *textually*, that there has been such resistance. De Man's identification of the *resistance to theory* is, in the rhetorical manœuvring of this fragment, also a resistance to acts of reading, where the *act* and *reading* name a certain response to the other ungovernable by any programme. Does this then imply that *reading* can be equated with *theory*? Is the former a synonym (of sorts) of the latter? Or do these terms relate to one another only in that manner of that *non-symmetrical and non-totalizable relation* discussed by Simon Critchley? Is there discernible a certain *rhetorical displacement* as the effect of reading *the resistance to theory*?

What should be clear by now is that what interests me here, throughout every twist and turn, detour and return concerning reading, is this issue of theory and, implicitly, that which de Man names *the resistance to theory*. If, as we have already seen, that which goes under the name *theory* is/was read from particular perspectives as merely formalist in its orientation   *not political, or at any rate not political enough, never political enough*   as Geoffrey Bennington suggests, then, from the other side, so to speak, that side which is observed by Paul de Man from where resistance is organised and projected, *theory* might be read as being *too political*.[27] As an ensemble of reading practices or acts, *theory* went, and continues to go, beyond the bounds of that which constitutes reading, through the insistence, on different occasions and in different voices, in asking political questions. In this we might read, once more, the translation from one question to another, where *what is it to read?* becomes translated as *what is to be done?*

Of course, *theory* does have a particular institutional history and identity, peculiar to Anglo-American universities, where it has come to be defined, identified. This is well known and much discussed.[28] The identification of 'theory', whether on the part of those who are in favour of 'it', or by those who resist, is in some measure an act of reading which has stopped. *The resistance to theory*, which is still there – and there, and there – is, in so many ways, and before anything else, a resistance to reading, as de Man makes plain. Moreover it is, clearly enough, a political resistance, inasmuch as the gesture of obstruction is constituted through resistance to reading in particular ways. Those whose voices are organised in this manner, whose commentaries stop short of reading, or who read with a kind of journalistic haste,   *a very sloppy kind of shorthand that the academic institution not only tolerates but prefers and proliferates*   are not only resisting readers if they are even this. They are, as Shoshana Felman makes clear, **resisting reading**   *resisting reading for the sake of holding on to our ideologies and preconceptions*   reading is displaced, brought to a violent halt by the assumption that what is termed within the institution *theory* and what Paul de Man calls reading *textually* has been read and, therefore, should not be read, should no longer be read, should never be read again, unless within carefully prescribed parameters (see n. 28).

Such resistance to reading, while no doubt having something of the affirmative, not to say evangelical aura, about its oppositionality, is, nevertheless, if not wholly, then certainly in some measure, an act of surveillance, structured by negativity and prohibition, which speaks the words – that is not good reading, we want nothing to do with it.

That second clause is performative. It demands that others do as they are told.

You shall have nothing to do with *theory*.

You shall not read *theory*.

You shall not read in the manner of *theory*.

You shall not read.

All of this is familiar, undoubtedly. Yet in the face of not reading, and in the face of the prohibition against reading in various ways which manifests itself in the shape of resistance, naming reading *theory* so as to displace reading with greater economy and efficacy, it bears repetition. Despite the familiarity, the asymmetrical transport between reading/not-reading remains in operation. If you are reading this, you are no doubt situated on the left of the divide. ('Left' in this case refers to a purely spatial relationship, not necessarily to a political determination.) If you are not, in any sense of not-reading, you're not.

This is all merely reorientation, albeit necessary if only so that we can return to reading and, in particular, reading *textually*   *'What is to be done?' must acknowledge the force of writing, its metaphoricity and its rhetorical discourse, as a productive matrix*   if we are not to be forced into the position of idle, and accused, readers. Found guilty of reading *textually*, we would be sentenced to be plunged into idleness.

De Man's response to the question of resistance is to describe exactly that which shifts the ground, and so displaces rhetorically, tropologically, figuratively, all anticipation of definition which it is the operation of resistance to produce. His description requires that we read the displacement at work in the first sentence of the fragment, so that what is resisted is exactly that *rhetorical or tropological dimension which can be revealed in any verbal event when it is read textually.* The sentence is frequently in danger of slipping away altogether, as it modifies and transposes its attention, situating, defining, rejecting definition, pausing parenthetically to prepare for the final statement, where *any verbal event* is in some measure a non-synonymous substitution[29] for that object of institutionally approved reading, *literature*.[30] In this wayward sentence, *literature* operates in at least two opposing directions, and it is precisely the displacement within the term which we need to read, in order to see how, in being the contested ground on which the struggle for reading occurs, the word needs to be read as a figure which disfigures.[31] There is perhaps most immediately available the narrow sense of the word, especially given the context within which reading is being discussed. *Literature* names narrowly forms of writing, whether poetry or prose, fiction or essay, which have been judged to have an established and, perhaps, even unequivocal aesthetic value. It has been read and subsequently judged of being suitable for further reading – though only in a specific custom. Nevertheless, *literature* can also be read as naming the movement of writing in a more general way.

Reading this contest between a more restricted and more open value for the term *literature*, we would suggest that the necessity for reading *textually* could be located here. There is installed the (dis)figuration of displacement which de Man argues for in the face of the *resistance to theory*. It is this displacement which *resisting readings* are incapable of reading, which institutes within the reading that resists, the resistance of reading, the resistance to what remains to be read. Displacement within *literature*, displacement from and within itself as a supposedly univocal identity, offers a glimpse of what reading might effect. It performs the slippage we named earlier the non-synonymous substitution: from *literature* to *any verbal event*.

Which is already a translation, where *any verbal event* is already silently written into *literature*, and which is what slips away, even as we attempt to grasp it. If we are to begin to be 'good readers', we must at least acknowledge that which always slips away, in that very moment when we believe reading has taken hold.

I am seeking the good metaphor for the operation I pursue here. I would like to describe my gesture, the posture of my body behind this machine. […]

What he would support with the greatest difficulty would be that I assure myself or others of the mastery of his text. By procuring – they say, distyle {*disent-ils*} – the rule {*règle*} of production or the generative grammar of all his statements.

No danger stepping there {*Pas de danger*}. We are very far from that; this right here, I repeat, is barely preliminary, and will remain so. (No) more names, (no) more nouns. It will be necessary to return to his text, which watches over this text here during its play.

So I am seeking the good movement. Have I constructed something like the matrix, the womb of his text? On the basis of which one could read it, that is, re-produce it?

No, I see rather (but it may still be a matrix or a grammar) a sort of dredging machine. From the dissimulated, small, closed glassed-in cabin of a crane, I manipulate some levers and, from afar, I saw that (*ça*) done at Saintes-Maries-de-la-Mer at Eastertime, I plunge a mouth of steel in the water. And I scrape {*racle*} the bottom, hook onto stones and algae there that I lift up in order to set them down on the ground while the water quickly falls back from the mouth.

And I begin again to scrape {*racler*}, to scratch, to dredge the bottom of the sea, the mother {*mer*}.

I barely hear the noise of the water from the little room.

The toothed matrix {*matrice dentée*} only withdraws what it can, some algae, some stones. Some bits {*morceaux*}, since it bites {*mord*}. Detached. But the remain(s) passes between its teeth, between its lips. You do not catch the sea. She always re-forms herself.

She remains. There, equal, calm. Intact, impassive, always virgin.

Jacques Derrida, *Glas* (1986, 204–205b)

Seeking to be the good reader, Jacques Derrida searches, appropriately, for the *good metaphor*, perhaps the most appropriate metaphor, that metaphor which most economically appropriates the text of Jean Genet, in the process of reading.[32] More than this, the *good metaphor* is that which most particularly approximates or describes the attempt to read. How then, to read reading? How to pursue the reading of a reading sensitive to the text of the other?

The *good metaphor*. The *good movement*. Metaphor, metaphoricity, propels. It transports. It also reads and, having read, translates. Reading: as metaphor: as movement. This is performed in this passage, in the passage between figures, between two figures, from one to the other, as we read the initial movement of a self-reflexive, self-questioning writing, seeking to locate itself as the reading it desires to become. We read the attempted orientation, the positioning of reading in its efforts to counter-sign Genet's text, to inscribe the act of reading within the text being read. Within the text of the other, and also, simultaneously from some other place, the other of the text, reading is already underway, in that search, that process, which is not itself but already the transport of the metaphor, its movement. There has been a movement already between writing and reading. From writing to reading, from metaphor to movement (metaphor *as* movement), in the movement of reading's machinery, and in the machine of reading's movement. Which is, of course, nothing other than to find oneself already underway in metaphor.[33]

From being behind the machine, the reader moves closer, appearing to repeat himself, at least in part, and, with this gesture, offering the counter-signature of construction which is reading. Construction is, we read, necessary to reading; more than merely an appropriate metaphor, it is intrinsic to the process. Construction belongs to reading read as a re-productive structure or organ. Machine. Movement. Matrix. Womb. Technicity and organicity. The reading act is implicitly gendered through its attempted efforts to insert itself in the equally gendered text of the other, in order that reading may reproduce, from within the other's text, an image of the other in the image of itself. And yet, as if to deny the organic process, there is, we read, that insistence on the hyphen in 're-production'. As if reading could divorce itself from its violation of the other's text by insisting on its purely mechanical re-generation. As though the text of the other had nothing to do with the process. Yet as the structural figure of the matrix affirms, the other's text is female, and from this other place, the place of the mother, reading is engendered. Reading reproduces itself – dream of autoeroticism – and, in turn, reproduction is a reading. Every metaphor thus far searches after one location; every figure transports the reader in one direction: towards the self-(re)generative movement of reading itself.

But this is only preliminary. The gendered assumption of reading is rejected for slipping into the hasty predictability of a bad reading, no doubt. How, though, to proceed in reading, to maintain the movement of a reading, retaining also the good metaphor? How to work within the movement, so as to enter the textual corpus, and to come away again, without succumbing to the violence of re-production?

The metaphor of the dredging machine might appear to be a somewhat curious, perhaps even awkward choice at first for describing the process of reading, but to read the power of this image, its strange and estranging forcefulness, its strength is not to be denied. The force of the image is such upon the reader who seeks to read through this passage of Derrida's own search, his own passage, that the effect of this image is best read not as being merely metaphorical but, more forcefully, as an example of catachresis. The exchange, the transportation between the idea of reading and the idea of dredging is so forceful as to estrange, defamiliarise, denaturalise, any assumed relationship between self and (m)other (which metaphor is, after all, in operation in this passage). The dredging machine does not belong to a re-productive technology. Its purpose is to transport, from one place to another. The act is violent, undoubtedly, but the question is one of translation, not generation. To imagine reading as dredging is to offer a wholly unfamiliar figure for a particular activity. This in itself forces us to consider the image as presented specifically through the operations of language, through the transference of metaphoricity itself. We are not allowed to assume that there is some more or less mimetic correspondence, we are prohibited in reading to lapse into a reading that is all too predictable, through that transformative and per-formative Derridean counter-signature as it struggles to come to terms with the (m)other's textual matrix (which figure of course figures already a double reading, a reading at once both organic and technological, resisting being read finally as residing solely on either side of the implied binarism).

Derrida follows through this image, describing how random articles are picked up as the teeth of the machine scrape the sea-bed. What gets held onto is not completely in the control of the act of either reading or reader. Something might be dropped, something remains, and much cannot be scooped up in the first place. Thus the image serves to suggest, in the struggle to come to terms with Genet, how no reading can ever gain mastery over the object of its enquiry. No reading can simply transport that being read in its entirety, preserving the identity of the other's text intact. What reading picks up, what it picks up on, cannot be wholly determined ahead of the event of the encounter. At the same time, whatever reading does gather, there is always that which remains. There are always the remains of reading, that which remains also as that which is not yet read. There is in the text of the other, beyond the tracing of any textual matrix, an excess or supplement beyond the act of reading.

The figure of the dredging machine is appropriate therefore to reading inasmuch as it cannot translate form and content from one place to another without loss, without slippage, without the remainder or excess. There is that which resists the appropriation of reading. This is put into play within and across language. Not only is there that Latin mother, the matrix so figured, there is also the mother and the sea in the homophonic oscillation of *Mer/Mère* which the translators, in order to approximate the double-reading within Derrida's passage, retain in French. The location in which Derrida chooses to imagine the staging of a possible reading, Saintes-Maries-de-la-Mer, is no accident, surely. For in that image of the mother who cannot be caught, who reforms herself, this mother the sea, do we not begin to read the figure of the Virgin Mary? However we might believe we catch a glimpse of such a possibility, certainly Derrida reads the futility in believing one can read, once and for ever.

If reading has historically been a tool of revolutions and of liberation, is it not rather because, constitutively, reading is a rather risky business whose outcome and full consequences can never be known in advance? Does not reading involve one risk that, precisely, cannot be resisted: that of finding in the text something one does not expect? The danger with becoming a 'resisting reader' is that we end up, in effect, *resisting reading*. But resisting reading for the sake of holding on to our ideologies and preconceptions (be they chauvinist or feminist) is what we tend to do in any case.

Shoshana Felman, *What Does a Woman Want?* (1993, 5–6)

To admit to the image of reading as always leaving something behind, of being unable to grasp at everything, will worry some and infuriate others. Clutching at straws, doubtless there would be those who would resist reading Derrida's search for the *good metaphor*, seeing in this instead a bad metaphor for reading. Writing Derrida's metaphor off without having read *textually*, without having begun to read the textual *matrix* in which such a metaphor inevitably involves itself as that disfiguring figuration which displaces the purely *grammatical cognition*, and which lets fall, and which lets remain, everything else; such a writing off, we suggest, is a resistance *to* and *in* reading. Such resistance to reading resists also a question of taking risks.

The good reader takes risks. Reading entails risk. It is an act which takes risks, which is itself risking everything in the event of reading, because reading opens itself to the other, and to the chance encounter with tex-tuality. This is why reading of a certain kind, whether reading to escape, reading guiltily, reading *textually*, or reading while acknowledging that there are remains and that no mastery over one's subject is possible, finally, is referred to as an act or an event. The act or event of reading is risky precisely because nothing is decided ahead of the event. Reading should not bring with it a programme or method, but should, instead, proceed step by step.

In this way, reading not only opens itself, it remains open to the force imposed upon it by the structure of the text, that which causes the reading to *swerve*. Thus, it might be said, reading must involve itself in and be constituted by a politics of openness, as well as by a politics of the opening. Such a politics would no doubt be altogether a much more open and, therefore, risky affair than that reading which is, as we have seen, either the manifestation – or, perhaps, the manifesto – of a *resistance to theory*; or, to take the other example, a *reading-towards-socialism*, which is, arguably, precisely the opposite of a politics of openness in being so governed by and directed towards an *eschatoideological* instance of arrival.[34]

In both examples just given, and previously considered, there is, albeit in highly individualised and different ways, the very opposite of either risk or openness (and being open necessitates risking oneself). It is not simply enough to say that the *resistance to theory* or *reading-towards-socialism* are both examples of not-reading or the limits of reading, although they are, when read from certain perspectives. Rather, both examples, and others like them, are often expressions of the negotiation between reading and not reading, and between reading within limits and towards a limit. Though ostensibly different, and articulating within conventional discur-sive parameters a politics of the Right and of the Left, both *resistance to theory* and *reading-towards-socialism* operate according to an economics of reading, where reading is organised according to the Law of the House.

Thus, the very risk of taking risks in reading, in being open to that which is unreadable ahead of the event or in the very act itself, is that very place where reading must read its encounter with the limit, which occurs all too often in the name of the limit we know as politics. While politically motivated reading of a revolutionary or oppositional nature has come about *historically*, as Shoshana Felman puts it, because of the desire to confront the limit, this has frequently resulted in the redefinition, the reconstruction, and the reintroduction of limits.

Yet the risk which cannot be avoided is the encounter with, and the consequences of, that which *can never be known in advance*. There is always the chance of coming face to face with that which, in the event of reading, will disarm all protocols, all programmes, all methodologies, all self–circumscribing modes of exegesis   *finding in the text something one does not expect*   we cannot account for this, nor can we anticipate it, and it is precisely this in/conceivable encounter which we hazard every time we read. Felman's fragment gives us to understand the risky double-bind in which reading places us, in our relation, as readers, to the text, to textuality in general. While we can conceive the likelihood of *finding in the text something one does not expect*, nevertheless, we cannot conceive what, exactly, it is we will find. We will never be able to resist the unimaginable.

Yet, if reading is proscribed ahead of the act, as a general principle by which a community of readers, so–called, agrees at what point reading is to be resisted, the unexpected, which *can never be known in advance*, can be, if not avoided, then denied. Felman's imagined *resisting reader* can *in effect, resist reading*. We have already seen this at work, and not only in the examples of the *resistance to theory* or *reading-towards-socialism*, which may be read, coincidentally, as offering a dualistic model akin to Felman's own examples of the *chauvinist or feminist*.[35] This effect of *resisting reading* has been there from the very beginning, because of *ideologies and preconceptions*, but for a host of other reasons also. It is remarked by Althusser in his acknowledgement that reading was not carried out, as *economists, historians, philologists*. It is named by Barthes *the literary institution*, where, he informs us (as will be recalled) reading *is nothing more than a **referendum***. The *resisting reader* who, together with other *resisting* readers, comes to offer a *resistance to theory*, demanding nothing less than an excuse for reading, or what Bhabha describes as *a pure teleology of analysis whereby the prior principle is simply augmented … its identity … consistently confirmed. Resisting reading* desires not only constant confirmation but what Derrida gives the name of *mastery*. And what this comes down to is the question of what it means to read   *it is again a question of the other*   *the event in poetry, meaning* *and inscription which escapes human control*   what we read in Felman's commentary is how the movement of reading, when subsumed by the movement of politics, or, more dangerously, the political movement, comes to a halt. No longer in motion, reading stops.

Seneca stresses the point: the practice of the self involves reading, for one could not draw everything from one's own stock or arm oneself by oneself with the principles of reason that are indispensable for self-conduct; guide or example, the help of others is necessary. But reading and writing must not be dissociated ... If too much writing is exhausting ... excessive reading has a scattering effect ... By going from book to book, without ever stopping, without returning to the hive now and then with one's supply of nectar – hence without taking notes or constituting a treasure store of reading – one is liable to retain nothing, to spread oneself across different thoughts, and to forget oneself. Writing, as a way of gathering in the reading that was done and of collecting one's thoughts about it, is an exercise of reason that counters the great deficiency of *stultitia*, which endless reading may favour.

Michel Foucault, 'Self Writing' (1997, 211)

The fear of reading, the anxiety produced in the face of the unreadable and the prospect of reading-to-come, is related to a fear concerning identity. The acts of reading which call a halt to reading's motion are either explicitly or implicitly concerned with reading up to a point. That point is the constitution of the subject or the subject's identity, whether by identity we mean the individual reader or a reading community seeking to define itself.

Michel Foucault stresses the point in providing a commentary on Seneca: situating or orientating the self and its construction involves reading. He makes this point, furthermore, in relation to an act of writing, which is, itself, part of the process of reading he describes. In this process, writing gathers reading, which, according to Seneca, when pursued in too desultory a fashion becomes excessive and scatters or fragments the self. Does this fear of excess not name the fear of endless reading which is encountered in what is named the *resistance to theory*, or in those who are named *resisting* readers, who resist *reading*?

The very idea that one could read too much is itself a construction, or, perhaps, an alibi, for calling a halt to the act. Reading must desist for the good of the self. The idea that reading might prove to be *excessive* suggests the fear of an overflowing of limits. Behind this figure of *excessive reading* is a utilitarian anxiety. What happens to what we have read, if we do not put it to some use? What happens to all that reading, if we fail to perform like the worker bees Foucault imagines, transforming our reading into writing? Reading has to be put to work, has to be translated into a writing, as a means of curbing excess.

Excessive reading is not the only name given to the fear. It is also termed *endless reading. Gathering. Collecting. Taking. Exercise.* These words name the imposition of limits on reading, limits which suggest a form of economism, of self-disciplining, and self-organisation. The self has to be placed within, subjected to, a regime wherein reading is curtailed and made to perform for a purpose, the purpose of giving meaning to the self. Otherwise, the self is scattered. The subject is spread *across different thoughts*. Unable to keep everything in mind, incapable of retaining all that is deemed an excess – and thereby speaking indirectly, without definition, of an appropriate amount, the right measure, so to speak – the self will *forget oneself*. Too much reading makes one *forget oneself*. The self is liable to be lost in the textual field, consumed by the other. Seneca's anxious recommendations for self-discipline appear to anticipate the very possibility of *escape*. There is a sense behind the precautionary prohibitions concerning too much reading that what must be avoided at all costs is the risk of the unexpected.

Anticipating excess means to anticipate the effacing of the self's limits, and thereby circumvent this through the *gathering in* that is writing. While this speaks of a certain possible dissolution of a purely psychic subjectivity (the self itself overflows, overflowing itself through the encounter with the textual excess), the metaphors of *gathering, collecting, exercise, taking* figure a predominantly physical activity, with which writing might be aligned. Reading, on the other hand, how might we define that? As a mental process? Certainly. But there is also the encounter between the self and the object that we call the book, which is in part physical. To read is both an act and an action. It already crosses boundaries, and cannot be confined solely by a definition which describes only physical or psychic activity. It involves both aspects of the self and thus, in engaging the self, denies either an isolated meaning free from the other.

The effect of *excessive reading* is to produce in the self not only that scattering, the fragmentation and dispersal of selfhood, but also, and especially, a specific form of the deregulation of the self. Too much reading or reading of the wrong kind makes you lose reason. What excess of reading points to, then, is not simply excess, that is to say, *too much reading*, but all reading pursued without its eventual subordination to routines of regulated, productive physical activity. It is not that there can be too much reading or something called *excessive reading*, as distinct, say, from reading within limits (even though this is the Senecan scenario as the excuse for the self's policing of reading). Instead, we must read that *all* reading *is* excessive.

However,

It is not certain that talking about fragmentariness brings one closer to it. The depiction of several fragmentary states is perhaps a better approach than the attempt to define the fragment as an object, but then only if one does not avoid the question of the relationship of such states to the reading of fragmentary texts. ... The anonymous, posthumous endlessness of the person who waits or who is sad is also the condition provoked by the fragment. The fragment is the text that one falls out of.

The fragment is unreadable: it has not been read when one takes notice of what is there nor can one read more than what is there. The fragment is fragmentary because it says less than it should. Something is not there, and this lack must be read as well. This is why it is not possible to talk about the fragment without also talking about what is not there. In the face of the fragment a basic methodological rule for rigor in speaking about texts fails: the rule that what is said must be corroborated by the text, must stand its test ... This fragmentary experience, as an experience of frag- mentariness, is not negative but neutral. In it the lack is not negation of fullness ... the lack is here opaque emptiness without opening, without extension or end, without a view on an opposite: exterior.

This experience belongs to the reading of the fragmentary text if the text is read as such. That is, in its breaking off, and if this is still reading. I read the text, but how do I read its stopping short? This event is not told, it just happens ... The text breaks off precisely to the extent that its stopping cannot be explained through what is there. Nevertheless the moment when the fragmentary text breaks off also belongs to one's experience of it, an experience that does not stop at the breaking point but outlasts it.

Hans-Jost Frey, *Interruptions* (1996, 48–9)

> *it is not certain that talking about fragmentariness brings one close to it.*

If the self is revealed as fragmented through reading ...

– Wait   *but how do I read its stopping short?*   This is a formula which may be read either as *if reading reveals the fragmentation of the self* or *if the self's fragmentation comes about through the act of reading*; on which of these *fragments* shall we decide? Which is the more immediately readable? Are both, in being *fragments*, in fragmenting the formula, unreadable?

If the self is revealed as fragmented through reading, this is not to say that reading – *too much reading, excessive reading* – fragments, or that there is a point up to which reading may go before it fragments. The self is composed only of fragments, and the act of reading affirms the subject's *fragmentariness*. For this reason, it is necessary to comprehend how the *fragmentary experience of reading* serves to turn our reading back upon the construction of our identities as navigations between reading and writing performances. Understanding the condition of subjectivity as the exchange between readings and writings, we might begin to admit that the *experience of fragmentariness is not negative but neutral*. The observation of negativity is the manifestation of a reading.

Reading is always this, *the experience of fragmentariness*. It fragments and unveils fragmentation, citation, as inescapable. Reading can never extend beyond this condition. It only extends itself, extending and promising to attenuate itself, through its own movement, its own fragmentation as the promise of future (as) fragmentariness. *Anonymous, posthumous endlessness.* This is reading. This is what it means, to read.

In one way, we have done nothing other, so far, than to acknowledge this, through the response to the various citations and fragments which we have encountered herein. This will continue to be the case. This essay is already in ruins. The focus has been and will continue to be on the question of *what is it to read?* and this has been and will continue to be engaged through the *depiction of several fragmentary states* – and of fragments within fragments, one citation to another, in a varying rhythm of contrapuntal gestures. The reason for this is spelled out   *perhaps a better approach*   although such an approach doubtless involves risks. The most immediate is that of (the reading of) a banalisation of the subject through seemingly endless repetition, reiteration, the constant return of commentary which seems to say what the fragment, what *fragmentariness* as *absolute construction*,[36] already seems to say, and, also, not to say, being incapable of saying it (hence our recognition of the fragment, the ruin).

It is of course necessary, if we are to proceed in this fashion, to acknowledge the *relationship* between the *several fragmentary states* of the self or the text and the act of attempting to read the *fragmentary text*, as

Hans-Jost Frey observes. If reading is read as an endless process, so also must the reading subject. Always already *riven* and caught up constantly in the citational to-and-fro, like the shuttle on a loom, or the ebb and flow of textual currents, to ask *what is it to read?* is to mark the return of the citation as that which haunts us, and to return *to* the fragment in a doubling movement, which, instead of constructing a unity,   *the attempt to define the fragment as an object*   produces instead the effect of desistance within the search for unity as the disorganisation of the search into fragments. To ask the question *what is it to read?* is to speak of what is absent, what is constituted by *lack*, and to situate the *fragmentary experience as an experience of fragmentariness*.

But, and this is the paradox, whereby reading, or, more accurately, the desire to read, is propelled, while this essay has not yet begun to read *and* has already, also, said too much …   *the fragment is unreadable*   seeing the fragment, constructing from the fragment what is lacking; this, says Frey, is not reading. (In passing, however, it should be noted that Frey's sense of not-reading is of a different order than those instances of not-reading spoken of elsewhere.) The *fragment* is *fragmentary*. If this remark seems unnecessary, unnecessary because so obvious, it *is* necessary to see how the fragment, although it may be readable as an *absolute construction*, is nevertheless never capable of being reassembled whole and intact. Our experience of the fragment is *fragmentariness* itself, in that it resists reading, construction, ordering. The fragment *remains* (to be read), and, in being unreadable, remains as the remains of reading, that which *escapes* or *exceeds* the idea, the dream of reading. *It says less than it should.*

But is this not a strong reading? Does this not determine, in reading reticence, an identity for the fragment? The reticence of the fragment, when read as such, suggests that one takes notice of what is there and *not* there, one seeks to accommodate both aspects and resolve them into a seamless form. This is not a moment of slippage in Frey's text, so much as it re-marks the *risk* involved in coming to terms with reading and, more significantly, the unreadable, that which *remains*.

To talk *about what is not there.* Does this effort to acknowledge the fragment run the risk of initiating a reading of *more than what is there*? The lack; or, better, *lack*, without the definite article, so as to avoid the implication that what is lacking can be identified and supplied; or, better still, ~~the~~ lack: retain the definite article, but place it under erasure, if only so as to determine that which is lacking is specific according to the text being read. So: ~~the~~ lack, specific aporia determined by the fragment as a condition of its non-unitary status, and neither some general lack (never that), nor some 'thing' which can be supplied. This term names, for Frey, some *opaque emptiness*, which is incapable of being opened, that is to say, being filled in by being read – and written (about? over? on? in?). Whether or not ~~the~~ lack is this expression or experience of *exteriority*, so-called (about which we remain in doubt as to the possibility of a pure exteriority, though unable to comment further at this juncture), in being read as such, as ~~the~~ lack specific to each fragment, it finds itself re-marked in two directions: without *extension* or *end*.

~~The~~ lack is thus marked by that movement peculiar to the idea of *clôtural* structurality, which is named *transgression* and *restoration*. Being without *end*, *infinite*, it moves endlessly, as the expression of a radical alterity of any *fragment* – which is to say any text, any textual structure, any text read *textually*. At the same time, ~~the~~ lack cannot be extended, even though it is without end; even while it exceeds itself as finite structure available to finite reading, reading within limits or towards a limit. It cannot be extended because within the framework that Frey compre-hends reading, ~~the~~ lack cannot be read when reading becomes the prosthesis of ~~the~~ lack which supplements it, which fills in for ~~the~~ lack. Neither simply there nor not there, ~~the~~ lack names that which is unreadable in the fragment, as well as that which constitutes the *fragmentariness* of the fragment without being constructive itself in any affirmative or positive sense.

The experience belongs to the reading of the fragmentary text if the text is read as such. The question of ~~the~~ lack comes down to the question of the act or event, unanticipated and uncontrollable. We are turned away from reading even in the event of the fragment's return. The event of reading, *in reading*, makes itself known in that moment proper to every text, which is nothing other than its breaking off, its *breaking point*, its *becoming-fragment*. This is the experience of every reading. And, if the experience is comprehended, there comes the *breaking point* of the textual thread in the comprehension of what constitutes reading   *what is it to read?*   so that if we are to *escape* or *exceed* the feeling of intran-sigence, intransitiveness, institutionalisation, if we are to comprehend the *remains* as unreconstitutable, then we must ask whether *this is still reading* if, by this fraught and fraying word, *reading*, we find ourselves unable to get beyond the writing effect which seeks to gather, to collect, to reassemble, and thereby ignore, efface or downplay all that we cannot master. Without giving up on reading, how are we to seek out the contours of an act of reading whereby we can admit that there is the instance of fragmentation where reading breaks off, and which also, in the experience of this moment, *outlasts it*?

For even before the reading reproduces the sense of absolute knowing, whether affirmatively or *ex negativo*, through its supplementary inter- pretive addition to the text, the reading in question has already entered the circle of the text, already become an immanent moment of its movement. ... And even before the reading becomes what it already is, even before it enters the dialectical circle of cognition, even before the active consciousness grasps itself at work there, this reading is still not yet what it already is, still halts before the threshold of its origin and falls short of its destination, arrives too early – and too late – for itself and its consciousness, and thereby opens out its hermeneutic-dialectical circle into a parabola. Although the reading does not approach its text in an external fashion, it is not yet the immanent movement of self-reproduction which it already is. The reading ... must commence from the not yet in the unity of the not yet and the already present: at a remove from that unity of arche and telos which would constitute the finally successful reading itself as identical with the system of absolute self-consciousness. For the dialectical logos the reading remains an endless foreword, one which transforms the logos into an anticipation of itself and without which that logos could not exist; a supplementary addition which reveals the final conclusion always already drawn by the system to be open after all. The reading introduces its 'self' into the circle of synthesis as a difference that cannot be synthesized.

This difference, which has both logical and phenomenological, structural and temporal determinants, is the condition for the reproduction of the text in its reading, and through those traits of delay, of remainder, of anticipation which it introduces into every act of interpretation, this difference presents the dialectical operation of reading with an insuper- able obstacle at the very entrance to the dialectical circle: an incorrigible deviation from meaning's path and process of meaning towards itself.
[...]
A reading which wishes to elude the suction of the dialectical circle as far as possible, in order to put itself in a position to descry the structure and dynamic of this circle, must begin precisely from these remnants of its own activity in the text, from that which it is not yet itself, or which it no longer itself is. It must begin, therefore, not merely from the logical structure and the systematic implications of such remnants, but also from the meta- phoricity of the text and the phantasmic dimension which is at work in it, from the as it were literary character ...

Werner Hamacher, Pleroma: Reading in Hegel (1998, 3–5)

It is important to discern the double, contradictory movement of reading, that which is revealed in the event and yet which, it must be admitted, is, after a fashion, always already installed, *textually*, so to speak, and which is also *not yet*. This is expressed in the following disorientating formula, which indicates a constant oscillation, perhaps the articulation of an *idling effect*, between an unspecified proximal past and a future to-come, neither of which can be resolved into a present, or reduced to a stabilising centre: *Reading is still not yet what it already is*. The temporal and spatial disruption of this phrase makes it (partially readable as) almost unreadable. Structured around the immanence, the glimpse, and the promise of reading, it nonetheless resists becoming that which would be most desired: a calm(ed) and calming supplementary analytical commentary, which would not only have moved beyond the text but would also have assumed a position outside the text prior to reading (as though such a thing were possible).

Reading is still not yet what it already is. How to come to terms with the seeming paradox – which Werner Hamacher traces, follows, unfolds, and patiently lays out – for the readers of this passage? There is the reader already implied in the immanence of the *already is*. There is Hamacher, the reader who reads himself moving through the impossible figure of reading. And there are others. This phrase maps the doubling contours of the passage we have before us, a passage, which, we might add, is nothing other than the passage of reading, *in* reading, via *delay*, *remainder*, and *anticipation*.

The passage described and enacted by Hamacher is the passage in and through which passage is both summarised and enacted, although this is *not yet* a reading, being an *endless foreword*. The phrase announces the incalculable difficulties encountered in pursuing the very condition of reading. Reading takes time, but it is impossible to find the right time for reading, the appropriate rhythm.[37] Hamacher's phrase, *even before*, names the difficulty and assigns to reading the status of the *endless foreword*. At the risk of being reductive or too schematic, it is worth staying with this remark.

Even before. Here is the location of reading where the act is *still not yet what it already is*, otherwise reiterated as the *immanent movement of self-reproduction which it already is*, and named the *not yet*. Hamacher calls this a unity   *the unity of the not yet and the already present*   though this is, it has to be confessed, a strange unity, traced irreducibly by that double trait, a doubling which is also the division that structures all reading, disjointing ahead   *even before*   of any reading, reading/unreadability, as what remains to be read. *Even before* appears to mark a simple temporality, an *a priori* location of the dilemma written in the impossible structure of *not yet/already is*, or *not yet/already present*. Location, therefore, as dislocation, past *and* future, though neither as present, as we have already stated. For, if the *even before* seems to be the inscription of the *a priori* in returning to us ahead of the passage, it also displaces the apparently straightforward temporality of its statement in returning that which has yet to be recognised, which is *immanent* and *not yet*. Thus, if I am to admit the force of these two words, I must learn how to read that which is inescapable and, yet, which cannot be read. In doing so, I have to understand how the phrase announces *delay*, *deviation*, and *anticipation*. Such an understanding involves that written engagement *of* and *in* writing/reading, where the necessary and ineluctable trembling and contagion of reading opens the aporetic we name responsibility, and through which, in response, comes the equally necessary and ineluctable movement of repetition.

In attempting to read, we get nowhere, and yet there is movement somewhere else. *Even before* we have got to the end of this citation, which we have anticipated, we have got no further than the paradoxical dis/location of the *even before*, which always names a step backwards, before the idea of the beginning, while inscribing the temporality of an *always-yet-to-come*. Never external to the text, neither the programme by which we bring the text under control, nor the meaning rendered by the act of reading, *reading does not approach its text in an external fashion*. An *endless foreword*, reading remains that figure of difference-within, the Saying of the Other, which reading can never synthesise as such. It does not become itself. Reading cannot, in the form of the supplementary addition, complete and thus close the *hermeneutic-dialectical circle*. Nor, through the act of interpretation, can it utilise what remains, finally, as part of a movement of *meaning towards itself*. Reading's wayward movement deconstructs the *dialectical operation even before* the circular enclosure gets underway.

Realising all the problems, all the impossibilities, Hamacher nonetheless seeks for a reading movement which will find a motion appropriate to reading. Such a re-citation involves the consideration of *remnants*, *metaphoricity*, and the *phantasmatic*. Reading must begin again, *from the as it were literary character*. This expression, *as it were*, names, as it were, that which cannot quite be named. Yet it also signals that which, in its name, indicates through indirection that which is proximate to the trace, the remnant, the ruin, fragment or (what) *remains*, as it were. Were we to turn Hamacher's projection of a reading which eludes *the suction of the dialectical circle* towards his own text, we might discern the operation of *metaphoricity*, the *phantasmatic dimension*, the *literary character* in this singular and proximal remark: *as it were*.

This phrase installs movement, yet interrupts the flow, as it were.

Through the act of coming close, but in not being, exactly, the expression of *literary character* itself, in intimating that the expression (in this case, *literary character*, which is, itself, already insufficient, inasmuch as it is a non-synonymous substitution, a supplement, for *the metaphoricity of the text* and *the phantasmatic dimension*, none of which are, themselves, phrases which can govern the play at work in the semantic chain nor act as master terms) is not enough, never enough, never that exactly which impels, propels, and compels the act of reading, the phrase *as it were* opens that which is already under way, the movement of difference,   *it is not yet the immanent movement of self-reproduction which it already is*   while re-marking the excessive trace in language.

Consider also, momentarily, the metaphors of the text, several of which are structural or spatial. Circles, parabolas, entrance, obstacle, path. Such figures sketch for reading its own haunted or phantasmatic structure, where reading must navigate an unmappable topography, an impossible architecture or architexture. The circle and path particularly invoke the ghost of Heidegger and a certain structural configuration of the inescapability of the metaphysical.[38] The figure of the path suggests the figure of an eventual return to the house of meaning, despite delays or obstacles, where arrival is always already written into departure. *Not yet what it already is*, reading is both divided and suspended. This is its double-bind. However, to read the *as it were literary character* of those figures which seek to hide their figuration or metaphoricity in their appeal to *structure* and the *systematic*: are we not thereby placing ourselves in a certain relationship with the movement of the text, from within its contours? Reading circle, path, obstacle, entrance as the remnants of an inescapable structure, a structure in ruin, where the remains of structure remain to be read – herein is the possibility of acknowledging the to-come of reading, *as it were*. At the same time, however, these figures keep the secret of their figurality by placing themselves in plain view. If their secret is maintained, if they are not read as the remnants or ruins of the literary, then it has to be understood that the difficulty rests in the act of reading. We are taught to read in such a way within a certain discourse, named by Hamacher as the *hermeneutic-dialectical circle*, so as not to read this figurality. Seeing the circle for what it is, reading the *as it were literary character* of the figure rather than its *structural* or *systematic* truth, we reach the moment at least where we realise the necessity for leaving the path.

But what might it mean to call a work of fiction a swindle or a confidence trick? Is such a judgement even possible? What prejudgements or presuppositions would have to be in place before one could read to that conclusion? And if that conclusion is determined by presuppositions, has one even read anything at all in reading such a fiction? It is as if this text did nothing more than expose its divided trait in order to suspend it at the very limit of the reading act. The divided, suspended trait of reading *in* the text and *of* the text – for it is precisely this difference that is suspended – doubles every mark, at every step. That is what one has to read and at the same time that is what one cannot read. From the moment the reading is part of what is read, from the moment the divide holding them apart must be crossed ... then all calculations are opened onto the incalculable, that is, onto a certain future. *The Confidence-Man*, in this sense, comes to us, if it comes at all, from this future. Its temporality is that of an always-yet-to-come, and it issues what may be called literature's unlimited credit card.

Peggy Kamuf, *The Division / of Literature or the University in Deconstruction* (1997, 171)

The path is all too frequently circular. So much reading fails to comprehend this and, in so doing, falls back into the habitual round. Despite itself,
it involves and invokes prejudices, *prejudgements or presuppositions*. These
name reading in a violent fashion, while making excuses for the responsibility reading entails, *even before* the act is underway. It is not going too
far, we feel, to suggest that, as we have seen elsewhere, the excuse for
reading is found to be most especially the case when the reader, moving
towards a *conclusion* is completely – allegedly – innocent. Unaware that his
or her reading is structured around and mobilised by whatever *prejudgements or presuppositions* are already in place and which serve to construct
the path by which one proceeds, the reader is barred from entering
reading.

Let's not speak of the reader, though; double this. Imagine two readers,
if you will. Two fictions concerning two readers. The one, the reader who
arrives armed with a programme, in the guise, for the sake of the fiction,
of a route map, all the paths mapped out. The other, the reader who reads,
claiming all the while to have no map of reading, yet who has learnt the
route by heart, or, more precisely, has been taught the route without
realising that a model was being put in place.

First reader, first fiction: the reader who brings to the text a programme
or method which is learnt *as* one or the other, comes to reading–within–
limits with the intention at least to analyse in a particular manner, even if
that manner brings an eventual halt to reading. This is so well known that
it hardly bears repeating. (Yet, precisely because the situation is so familiar,
it needs to be reiterated.) Whatever happens during the encounter, however the text resists or subverts the programme, there is still the deliberate
engagement of that kind whereby predetermined results are expected on
the part of the reader who practises reading–within–limits, that reader who
reads towards a particularly rendered form, whereby the text is eviscerated
in the name of form. The eventual halt just indicated is written into the
programme or method prior to any reading.

Second reader, second fiction: the reader who claims, or believes, that
she or he has no programme or method, the one who reads 'simply for
pleasure', as the phrase goes, often resists the very notion that he or she
reads according to any *prejudgements or presuppositions*. Yet it is the case that
the reader is placed in a relationship to the text as a result of a complex
predetermination of aesthetic, economic, and cultural values, so loosely
organised as to be virtually inarticulable as such, except as they manifest
themselves or find themselves translated in the reader's enjoyment. This is
equally well known. However, such an analysis is resisted, and perhaps for
no other reason than that reading, being a matter of the constitution of
the self, cannot, or will not, read itself. Moreover, the reader of a certain

kind resists reading to that extent that reading itself needs to be read, and yet takes place everywhere, without the necessary doubling or reflexive turn.

In both fictions, the readers are identified, and perhaps identify themselves, through the limit of the act of reading. Both, in their own way, are *plunged into a kind of idleness*. Indeed, to the extent that the routes taken in reading and limiting reading are guided by *prejudgements or presuppositions*, whether conscious or unconscious, reading cannot be said to have been comprehended.

In this situation it seems as if we are as far as ever from beginning to answer the question *what is it to read?*, much less *what is to be done?* The situation is announced economically in the prefix: *pre*. It proclaims in a clear, loud voice that reading is already assured of its ending or *breaking point*. The end is always already in sight, de*termi*ned. To the extent that this is the case, as Peggy Kamuf asks – and that extent, by the way, is the *pre*sumption of the terminus, the limit once again, the judgement *avant la lettre* – has one even read anything at all in reading such a fiction?

The ostensible fiction here in question for Kamuf, that work prejudged or presupposed to be a *swindle or a confidence trick*, is Herman Melville's *The Confidence-Man*, as you can see. However, I want to read the question   *has one even read anything at all in reading such a fiction*   in a manner aimed at forcing the meaning of fiction in a slightly different direction, taking a detour, and reading, *as it were*, so as to give it a somewhat different inflection. This reading is already installed in the fragment above. I merely wish to tease it out a little, given that Kamuf calls our attention to what occurs when reading is called to a halt not only from the side of critical articulation but also as a result of that which the text puts into place and suspends.

Let us not presume that *fiction* or the phrase *such a fiction* refers only to a *work of fiction*, such as, for example, the example given, Melville's *The Confidence-Man*. Let us imagine, instead, that the *fiction* in question – such a fiction! – is what is produced in the event that the reading does not take place at all. At least, this is the direction in which I read Kamuf taking her readers. The *fiction* occurs when *prejudgements or presuppositions* produce what looks like a reading of sorts. The fiction in question is that definition of a *work of fiction* as a *swindle or a confidence trick*. This is the fiction produced by certain critical or analytical acts. This is the **work** *of fiction*, from one perspective, to produce for the text a teleological identity, to finish it off in the name of reading so as to break off from the text. *Fiction*, in this sense, names the direction of reading towards the suspension of reading   *the very limit of the reading act*   it describes fictitiously as it were the effect of prejudgement.

However, the question remains, what occurs if the text to which we assign an identity actively engages with the *work of fiction*, and, with that, the issue of what, how, where we read or do not read? If, on the one hand, the fiction of reading does *nothing more than expose its divided trait in order to suspend it at the very limit of the reading act,* how might a *fiction* trick us or trip us up, except by exposing reading – *in the text and of the text* – and thus producing that textual undecidability which comes from doubling? Such a figure, always already double, redoubles in the event that one attempts to read it. The figure of *fiction* or, to put this another way, the figurality of *fiction,* is this double gesture which, in its motion or rhythm, produces disfiguration through the disjunctive encounter and violent transformation that we call reading. *Fiction* names economically the doubling motion wherein *the reading is part of what is read,* where one both has to read and cannot read the *very limit of the reading act* and the *unlimited credit card* we call literature.

Two fictions, then,   *unlimited credit*   *the very limit*   though not simply opposites. Rather, each as the seemingly paradoxical internal necessity of the other, a doubling within and from itselves. (Not itself, never *itself,* but already doubled: *Not yet/already is.*) To seek to read this, to read the doubling of reading in this, is only ever to comment on the *trait,* on division, on that difference which both opens and which makes possible the comprehension of the opening. The one, in touching the other, opens undecidably at that point where the limit appears to have been (b)reached. In having opened the idea of fiction to the thought of its closure,[39] and thereby reopening it to itself in its very limit and suspension, we open onto the *incalculable* and *unlimited*   *a certain future*   wherein, what we term 'literature' addresses itself to the very idea of an open temporality named reading, *an always-yet-to-come.*

Why must we leave off reading only to return to it? What is its difficulty such that it does not simply frustrate us but instead incites us, regardless of our desire for simplicity, for the simplicity we associate with our selves, necessarily to return to what is impossible for us? What would reading be if we could do it, if we could finally succeed, stop this reading? This *sortie*, and its retraction, is no accident but rather the very condition of reading, in its necessity and impossibility.

[...]

There is no road for reading, no path or method: simply the effort and the fatigue of the difficult chance. As chance, reading and its inability defy calculation in advance, refuse prediction.

Thomas Keenan, *Fables of Responsibility* (1997, 92, 102)

The element of *chance* in reading should be not only that which we have to acknowledge, along with Thomas Keenan. It should also be recognised as a governing factor in the event of reading which disorganises all institutionalising and programming efforts.[40] *Chance* has led me to this point, in no small way, to the point where I experience simultaneously a double movement: acceleration and an ever greater meshing of gears. *Chance* has dictated the directions in which this essay has so far turned, the various *sorties* it has made, only to abandon them. Even the apparent matter of order, of the imposition of an order, has been decided on so as not to decide on the way in which reading should proceed, as far as this is possible (*necessity and impossibility*).

Taking a chance on the directions dictated by only the most basic order, I have sought to allow this writing to drift, as far as possible, keeping the act of reading open.[41] Drifting between signatures, citations, and fragments, remnants and ruins, this essay has sought to negotiate the various currents. Breaking off, stalling, only to acknowledge the chance of beginning again, and returning   *from the moment the reading is part of what is read, from the moment the divide holding them apart must be crossed … then all calculations are opened onto the incalculable, that is, onto a certain future*   Chance has to be maintained, if reading is to continue, if the reading act is a response, and undertaken responsibly.

Despite the persistence of the metaphor, *there is no road for reading, no path or method*. In spelling this out, Keenan does not so much move beyond Hamacher's comment   *an incorrigible deviation from meaning's path*   as he abandons all pretence of the path as a structure or route by which reading may pursue its goal or from which it deviates. Reading, in this reading, *and its inability* affirm waywardness, disorientation and the disjunctive encounter through which occurs transformation – of reading, of the self – as the affirmative resistance to the finally calculable, and to *prejudgements or presuppositions* or, indeed, *prediction*.

If there is a certain sense here of the text folding back upon itself, bringing the probability of reading to a halt in the act of a turn which also resembles a return (whereby we return to earlier issues, even in the doubling gesture of their return through the offices of reading to us), this is inescapably the effect of reading, as well as a sign of what it means to read responsibly   *what is it to read?*   *why must we leave off reading only to return to it?*   Repetition increases incrementally. It adds to itself in the process of reading, even as it displaces the effects read in earlier articulations. This is part of the inevitable and incalculable *chance* in which we involve ourselves *in* and *by* reading. It explains why, as Keenan puts it, we *return to what is impossible for us*. We seek out the contours of that which we desire to read and in doing so, counter-sign those features, those figures in an encounter which both transforms and doubles, lovingly and violently. Reading, which must proceed by chance, must begin by reiteration and, in so doing, disfigure for ever the make-believe, the *fiction*, of a beginning.

After a fashion, then, we could read in the remnant of Keenan's text the reiteration of a number of issues concerning reading already addressed, albeit in different ways, in different contexts. This would create the appearance of gathering together the threads, seeking to weave together disparate strands, so as to give a sense of unity. This in itself is a chance, but also the limitation of chance, where reading sets out (along the path?) to create the family atmosphere, the family resemblance.

Seduced by this possibility, we might wish to acknowledge that matter of *leaving off* and *return* as figured in Kamuf's text. This is noted there as that moment of division and its *suspended trait*, and the subsequent moment of crossing   *transgression?*   where *all calculations are opened onto the incalculable*. There might also be read here that instance of fragmentation, the *breaking point*, of which Hans–Jost Frey speaks. While Frey speaks of the fragmentary text, and fragmentation itself, there is that *experience* of the fragment which *outlasts it*, which can be named reading. It is for this reason that we return to reading. Our *experience* involves that which *does not simply frustrate us but instead incites us*. This double movement, of the moment and beyond, might also be named, after the image of **clôtural** *reading* proposed by Simon Critchley, *transgression* and *restoration*, of the leaving off and return, of the *necessity and impossibility*.

These threads can doubtless be picked up, woven together, transformed into what might be called a reading of reading, as though to simplify the task and thereby provide a sense of more or less stable identity. Such apparent simplicity is the *chance* we might give into, in the face of that other chance, *the difficult chance* which is reading without a *path or method*. It is that which Keenan suggests we desire, often in the face of reading's *difficulty*, its frustrations and the *fatigue* which it imposes. The simplicity we desire is far from simple. It is complicated by that ambivalence on the part of the reader, who stops and starts, in a shuttling motion,   *why must we leave off reading only to return to it?*   and returns to reading, motivated by that *simplicity* which reading, in truth, can never become. But the paradox is driven by the fact that the simplicity we desire to impose on reading, to put the breaks on so sharply that we come to a *breaking point*, is the simplicity we assume for our identities   *the simplicity we associate with ourselves*   we wish to read so as to simplify, to ignore the textile weave, to render reading into an undifferentiated totality. Reading-as-simplicity desires the production of an identity ignorant of alterity, ignorant of the difference which makes it possible,   *a difference that*

cannot be synthesized   doubling every mark, at every step   unenlight-
ned also concerning *the immanent movement of self-reproduction which it
already is.*

Nevertheless, because there can be no *prediction* or *calculation* which
reduces the chance by which reading proceeds, returns, stops, and starts,
again and again, simplicity in reading can never, simply, impose on reading
an identity which brings all reading to an end. Despite those feelings of
frustration and fatigue engendered by the continual unveiling of the
possibility or impossibility of reading

One must be able to stay nimble as one reflects, and stay on the 'surface' whilst reading between the lines. A task which requires one to elevate 'reading to the level of an art': there is no reading without interpretation, without commentary – in other words without a new writing which slightly displaces the meaning of the first, pushes the perspective of the aphorism in new directions and makes it come into its own. Every reading gives birth to a different text, to the creation of a new form: that is indeed an artistic effect. At the same time the text, the expression of a system of forces, acts on the reader and 'cultivates' him, in other words again it makes him come into his own. One must first of all be 'deeply wounded' and then 'secretly delighted' in order to be able to boast of having understood an aphorism: we can discover in a text only what we ourselves are but were unaware of. So reading transforms the reader and the text at the same time. ... A new reading/writing destroys the traditional categories of the book as a closed totality containing a definitive meaning, the author's; in such a way that it deconstructs the idea of the author as master of the meaning of the work ... The aphorism, by its discontinuous character, disseminates meaning and appeals to the pluralism of interpretations and their renewal: only movement is immortal.

Sarah Kofman, *Nietzsche and Metaphor* (1993, 116)

one must be able to stay nimble as one reflects, and stay on the 'surface' whilst reading between the lines. This resembles an aphorism: a definition of reading, perhaps, it remains difficult to read nonetheless.[42] Staying nimble, reflecting all the while, we should attempt to read the quotation marks with which Sarah Kofman suspends the metaphor of surface.[43] Those mute diacritical marks remark silently on the metaphoricity of the figure, separating it from its surroundings. Of course, the very idea of 'surface' implies depth, and from the perspective of certain readings, the depths are the place from which meaning is to be dredged, assuming that it is to be found there in the first place. However, this is to provide a dimensional model which, in fully activating the 'natural' operation of the metaphor, submerges the metaphorical   *the as it were literary character*   dimension (so that, in effect, the metaphor is sunk, out of sight). Suspending it above the waves of the text, as though the figure were caught in the teeth of some dredging machine (and this is very much an instance of seeking the right metaphor), Kofman insists silently that reading break off, in order that we read that which precisely remains unread: the artificiality of metaphor, its *literary* function. Without reading this, how can we hope to read at all? How can we offer either *interpretation* or *commentary*?

Furthermore, moved on from those quotation marks, we find ourselves at the very idea, the figure, of *reading between the lines.* Such a remark suspends reading in the ambiguity of its effect. A commonplace phrase concerning the nature of reading after a fashion, already used elsewhere by Homi Bhabha,   *a contradictory process of reading between the lines*   how are we to read this phrase? If the text is nothing but surface, so to speak, how do we navigate its matrix? After all, depth perception is necessary to orientation, or so we are led to believe. The phrase *reading between the lines* is a metaphor, the metaphoricity of which is all too readily understood and, therefore, not read at all. It addresses that which is not expressed in so many words and yet which is available as and in the *contra-diction* of reading. Staying *on the 'surface' whilst reading between the lines*: this phrase, operating through the force of metaphor, is structured around the implied contradiction of that *whilst*, which presents reading as the effect of the order of *on the one hand – on the 'surface'* – and, *on the other hand – reading between the lines.* The effects in play here are precisely that which reading has to take into account, without in any way reducing the play. It is a matter of *interpretation* or *commentary* which is attentive rather than reductive.

As there is no reading *without interpretation, without commentary,* so, clearly, there can be no reading without writing. Reading is simultaneously disjunctive *and* transformative. Effecting fraying and rupture, it 'becomes' that which it already is, immanently, while also being that which it is *not yet*. (As we know after Hamacher.) This is the effect *of* and *in* reading. It is also that which reading makes possible   *so reading transforms the reader and the text at the same time*

We have already comprehended this reduplication, though to speak of effect, of what may be effected, traces an act simultaneously in the text, immanently so, and by the text, which takes place in the act of reading. This is noticeable in the definition of text, described by Sarah Kofman as the *expression of a system of forces*. *Commentary, interpretation*, the definition is itself the reading of what reading causes to take place. This *expression* is read as that which *acts on the reader*. As she suggests, *it makes him come into his own*. This transformative condition, that which Paul de Man describes as reading *textually*, remarks the self. In doing so, it opens up the self to the division within itself, whereby reading's effect is to unveil the self as never simply itself, never the desired unity of undifferentiated selfhood,   *our desire for simplicity, the simplicity we associate with our selves*   but rather as being marked by that reading described as the *expression of a system of forces*.

There is partially readable here a difference between Kofman's consideration and de Man's understanding of text, which we might ascribe to an act of *reading between the lines*, and which, moreover, concerns a question of *the 'surface'*. While, for de Man, the *rhetorical, tropological*, and *figurative* effects of the text, when read, cause system and structure, logic or 'grammar' to be disfigured   *reading will be a negative process in which the grammatical cognition is undone, at all times, by its rhetorical displacement*   the effect is that which is either read or not read. Effect is read by de Man, in this instance at least, as remaining at the level of textual operation, even if reading moves elsewhere.

For Kofman, however, the act of reading transforms the text of the self also, which reciprocally manifests itself in the reading/writing of the text, narrowly conceived, as the book, the printed word, the essay. This is not to say that de Man is not aware, in other places, of the self as text, or that he does not read the self *textually*. However, and as a means of focusing on the doubling (of) effect, it is necessary to observe the extent to which Kofman makes explicit, through her reading of misreading in the text of Nietzsche, the unstoppable movement of reading as the effect of *misprision*, which makes reading, finally, so *impossible*, as it leaves its trace on the reader. This effect is remarked economically, as the figure of supplementary doubling, and in the movement − *of* and *in* reading − between text and reader, in the phrases: *makes it come into its own*; *makes him come into his own*. These remarks are not simply statements, observations on the function of aphorism in Nietzsche's text, they are already readings, acts of *interpretation, commentary*, which reduplicate the effect of reading, and which we are given to comprehend through Kofman's reiterated phrase, *in other words, in other words again*. This effect takes place throughout the fragment, at least from the seemingly aphoristic pronouncement that *there is no reading without interpretation, without commentary*. Inasmuch as this defines reading after a fashion, it also comments on, interprets reading. It thus affects even as it disseminates its effect.

It is tempting to read this remark as an aphorism, and, from this, to run the risk   *as chance, reading and its inability*   of enumerating the effects of reading aphoristically, as Kofman states them in the remnant, to read throughout the passage, and as the passage which reading opens, by which reading proceeds, a number of reading's ruins, aphorisms, and countersignatures:

> 🥀 there is no reading without interpretation, without commentary – in other words without a new writing which slightly displaces the meaning of the first
> 🥀 every reading gives birth to a different text, to the creation of a new form
> 🥀 at the same time the text, the expression of a system of forces, acts on the reader
> 🥀 we can discover in a text only what we ourselves are but were unaware of
> 🥀 so reading transforms the reader and the text at the same time
> 🥀 a new reading/writing destroys the traditional categories of the book as a closed totality containing a definitive meaning
> 🥀 the aphorism, by its discontinuous character, disseminates meaning and appeals to the pluralism of interpretations and their renewal.

Staying *on the 'surface'* of this text, the reading effect reiterates and reduplicates itself supplementally, performing its own discontinuous character. Kofman's text is readable as being organised and disorganised by the aphoristic nature of these commentaries, these readings of what it means, to read. Rhythmically punctuating the structure of commentary, they comment contrapuntally, and so countersign that discussion of reading of which they are a part. Reading assumes *on the 'surface'* the act, the performance, already implicitly underway. Each aphoristic reading – each reading of aphorism and each aphorism concerning reading – simultaneously suspends or arrests, while enacting the promise of the transgression beyond itself, its movement   *only movement is immortal*   figuring that temporality which *is that of an always-yet-to-come*. Reading these statements of Kofman's as aphorism, we learn to read aphoristically, reading for disjunction, disfiguration, heterogeneity. In reading these, we read the survival of reading, through *chance*, through repetition, and reiteration. This is reading in ruins, reading (as) remains.[44]

This *chance* is dictated in part by the infectious condition of Nietzsche's own ruined, ruinous text, as Kofman acknowledges elsewhere. Contamination is inescapable, especially when it comes to reading. As a result, reading or, at least, the desire to read can become uncontrollable.

Infectious *laughter* is catching, highly contagious, and ... almost impossible to bring under control. Likewise, I suspect, infectious reading.
David Farrell Krell, *Infectious Nietzsche* (1996, 197)

The idea that reading might be infectious produces laughter, doesn't it? Infection, derived, the OED informs its readers, from the Latin *inficere*, means to dip in, to stain, taint, spoil. The reader might dip into a book, so to speak, and become infected, contaminated, as something is transmitted. What gets transmitted? The desire to continue reading, perhaps. *Almost impossible to bring under control.*

The very idea that reading is *highly contagious*, and that a certain strain of reading, all too easily transmissible, can taint: is this not perhaps the fear that is named in that phrase of Paul de Man's, *the resistance to theory*? The first sign of the contamination of the reading-effect is a somewhat delirious joy, a destabilisation in the face of figuration, doubling, motion, all of which produce concomitant effects in the reader. One can imagine the diagnosis: the patient lost all sense of self through reading *textually*.

Doubtless there is a desire for escape, accompanied by laughter. There is quickly discerned a transmission between physical and physiological symptoms of reading, and from there to moral or mental depravity. There are those compulsions associated with *infectious reading* identified by Hélène Cixous. Those of us who are infected find that we are in the process of *pretending before the eyes of the family*. Every moment of reading occurs *on the sly*. We believe we are *eating the forbidden fruit, making forbidden love*. As Cixous says, *reading is doing everything exactly as we want and 'on the sly'*.

This all smacks of pathology and guilt, more than the hint of dissipation, of wasting the self. The self is *spread* as Foucault, in reading Seneca, puts it. Excessive reading exhausts. This is another of its symptoms. And it is no doubt a sign of reading's being excessive that, our resistances lowered, our immunity down, we become infected, and crave to spend ourselves further.

But herein is the Catch-22 of reading: the infection drives us on in our craving for the excessive, to be at once secretive, guilty, and yet, to flaunt our contaminated, depraved condition. Unable to stop, we *leave off reading only to return to it*. Its infection is such that it *does not simply frustrate us but instead incites us*. Caught up in *infectious reading*, we *return to what is impossible for us*. Reading courses through the body, and there is no cure. The extent to which the infection has taken hold is such that

Everything written today unveils either the possibility or impossibility of reading and rewriting history. This possibility is evident in the literature heralded by the writings of a new generation, where the text is elaborated as *theatre* and as *reading*.

Julia Kristeva, 'Word, Dialogue and Novel' (1986, 56)

everything written today unveils either the possibility or impossibility of reading.
We've heard this before. That the text is elaborated as both *theatre* and
reading,[45] this might be considered in some quarters scandalous, a sign of
infection, of physical disorientation and moral degeneration. That would
amount, however, to one of those *prejudgements or presuppositions*.

However, precisely because one wishes to avoid the closure of reading
to itself by such actions, it is desirable to read *between the lines*. In the
present case, we should recall the date of the citation's inscription – 1966.
Indirectly, acknowledging this date, or attempting to navigate a reading
which takes account of this year, we seem to be turning back on ourselves.
It appears that we are returning to the question of a starting point, and the
impossible location of a beginning with which to acknowledge the
inception of what has been described elsewhere as *guilty reading*.

Although not published until 1969, the *today* of 1966, of which Julia
Kristeva speaks, shortly after moving to Paris, is another possible
beginning concerning the matter of reading. This is at least as plausible a
narrative gambit as any of the others we have employed   *if we are to
speak of the question of reading, and to talk about this act of reading, moreover,
which does not assume itself to be innocent*   the date marks a moment
of crisis, perhaps, or at least it may be read in this fashion. The crisis
is negotiated in Kristeva's essay (from which the remnant cited above
comes), between a certain adherence to structuralism on the one hand,
and the recognition – on Kristeva's part through her engagement in the
essay in question with the subversive condition of language recognised in
the text of Bakhtin – of the necessity to move elsewhere on the other. This
negotiation can itself be read as the comprehension of a *breaking point* in
reading and a desire to return to reading, to return to reading the *difficult
chance*.

This is not simply Kristeva's crisis. We could read this as belonging to a
broader upheaval   *a symptom and a product*   the crisis, in the sense
of decision to be made in the event of confronting what reading entails,
is at work in 1966, not only in France, in Paris particularly, but also, in an
orientation, the co-ordinates of which would have to be fully discerned
and traced, in the USA, in the university. As a gesture towards a reading,
we might go so far as to say that an event took place in 1966 concerning
reading, the ramifications of which are still in effect, and which still have
yet to be read thoroughly, rather than with the journalistic haste both
within and outside the academy, which is still so much in evidence. The
event, perhaps describable as both *theatre* and *reading*, was a conference
at Johns Hopkins University, where Roland Barthes, Tzvetan Todorov,
Jacques Lacan, and Jacques Derrida, amongst others, were brought
together in the English-speaking academy for the first time.[46] The event

in question therefore bears the signs of negotiating with the radical rethinking of what it means to read, so as to translate the issue of radical reading into recognisable institutional forms.

This now well-known conference is, as we suggest, an instance of crisis and negotiation, specifically concerned with questions of reading and its impossibility, with reading as *theatre*, with text as *reading*   *where the text is elaborated as* **theatre** *and as* **reading**   yet something else occurs as a result of the confrontation between languages over reading. This is also well known, and a matter commented on elsewhere in this essay. It is, possibly, a matter of repression, the repression of reading and what that entails for the self (whether one speaks of the individual or the institutional self) in its desire for *simplicity*, and, with that, the evasion of *guilt*, of asking one's self, *what is it to read?*

Kristeva addresses this result, at the beginning of a talk given at another conference, this time in 1981, when she speculates on the repression of reading. *Academic discourse, and perhaps American university discourse in particular, possesses an extraordinary ability to absorb, digest and neutralize all of the key, radical or dramatic moments of thought, particularly a fortiori, of contemporary thought.*[47] Even in the instance of that *today* where *everything* interests itself in *what it is to read*, and where writing *unveils either the possibility or impossibility of reading and rewriting*; where, also, *the text is elaborated as* **theatre** *and* **reading**, there is also, retrospectively – that is to say available to a reading of sorts – the discernible signs of imposing limits on reading, that *extraordinary ability*, which Kristeva will identify fifteen years after the event. (It is interesting to note, in passing, that Kristeva retains the performative figure, speaking in the first instance of *theatre* and in the second of the *dramatic* moment.)

From one conference to another, then, as *chance* would have it. From a commentary on the opening(s) of reading, to another on its closure, its absorption, digestion, and neutralisation. But this is inevitable, conceivably, in the face of **infectious** *reading* or performance. (As an analogy, we could point to the repeated closures of the theatres of early modern London, on the grounds of the possible spread of infection.) The contagion has to be *neutralised*.

And at another conference, when Geoffrey Bennington speaks of the limits imposed on reading by a post-theoretical habit, he is, perhaps, doing no more than identifying the anti-body that was present within the institutional self all along   *Post-theory has often become a thinly made-up return to pre-theoretical habits*   in which there has been a renewed interest, in the name of reading. The contest for reading/not reading, reading to-come and reading within or towards a limit is the scene of both theatre and the treatment of contagion. Comprehending this, we see that it is not so much a question of reading a simple anterior moment, a reaction after the fact which that prefix *post* appears to identify. It must be a matter of reading the always present effort – implicitly traced in Bennington's acknowledgement of a *return to pre-theoretical habits* – to keep in check the theatricality of reading, and thereby to prevent it from spreading.

When Kristeva responded to the theatricality of reading over thirty years ago, had she a sense that the university was to become the theatre itself, a place for the enactment of a life and death struggle over reading itself? Did she envisage that the theatre was also an operating theatre, and that the, at times, very public excision of *infectious* reading would be attempted not only in the name of hygienics, but also with a flair for melodrama impossible to gauge?

What happens in Joyce's work? The signifier stuffs (*vient truffer*) the signified. It is because the signifiers fit together, combine, and concertina – read *Finnegans Wake* – that something is produced by way of meaning (*comme signifié*) that may seem enigmatic, but is clearly what is closest to what we analysts, thanks to analytic discourse, have to read – slips of the tongue (*lapsus*). It is as slips that they signify something, in other words, that they can be read in an infinite number of different ways. But it is precisely for that reason that they are difficult to read, are read awry, or not read at all. But doesn't this dimension of 'being read' (*se lire*) suffice to show that we are in the register of analytic discourse?

What is at stake in analytic discourse is always the following – you give a different reading to the signifiers that are enunciated (*ce qui s'énonce de signifiant*) than what they signify.

Jacques Lacan, 'The Function of the Written' (1998, 37)

To read the text as *theatre* is of course to respond to what takes place. The scandal for some is not so much in the reading of the performative dimension of textuality. Rather, it is in the fact that either they had not read it, or that the performative, the theatrical, was and is understood to challenge the mastery over the text upon which certain approaches to reading rely. Arguably, no text is more overtly theatrical than Joyce's. 'Theoretical' habits of reading do not impose this theatricality; they serve to activate it through the counter-signature of commentary and *analytical discourse.*

But to suggest that we *read* **Finnegans Wake**? Isn't Lacan having a laugh? Is anything less imaginable than that we *could* read Joyce's last text?[48] If only reading were that simple. If only it were not the case, which the Joycean performance makes so clear, that the text *can be read in an infinite number of ways*, opening itself in an *incalculable* manner, which announces the irreducible temporality of reading and, therefore, its impossibility. In the face of the Lacanian imperative, we have to acknowledge the following as conditions, chances, and effects of reading, all of which are not only the analyst's observations, but which also structure and displace reading – as translation – in Lacan, effecting a performance of that which Lacan addresses: slippage.

These conditions are defined as follows: *Difficult to read. Read Awry. Not read at all*. At the same time as we read in these phrases the problem of the analytical dimension and experience, we must also understand them as performative commentaries, on the texts of both Joyce and Lacan, where meanings and signifiers do go *awry*, are *difficult to read*, are *not read at all*. In commenting on Joyce, in directing us to read *Finnegans Wake*, knowing full well that this can never happen, that we can only ever remain *on the edge of reading Joyce*, as Derrida puts it; and, in speaking of the *chance* of listening and reading which defines for Lacan *what is at stake in the analytic discourse*; there is partially readable the difficulty experienced, again and again, in reading Lacan. There is always slippage, within one language, from one language to another, within the various languages or discourses which Lacan employs in so slippery a manner.

Difficult to read. Read awry. Not read at all. You will, doubtless, have noticed all of these related difficulties immediately at work in this ruin. You will have noticed it – read this fragment – most intensely in process in those pieces of parenthetical text, little entrails, all of which have to do, in one way or another, with reading,   *this dimension of 'being read'* **(se lire)**   there are, disruptively, within the text, those dislocating, disfiguring fragments which resist translation, announcing and situating themselves as ruins, the ruins of reading, and thereby signifying *something, in other words*. We are, we believe, in the presence of text (which enunciates itself) as *theatre* and *reading*. For, even as Lacan speaks of that which is *difficult to read*, his text is marked repeatedly, and internally – it comes to mark, to stuff itself – by those acts of signification which are, themselves, difficult to read, and which perform this *swerve*, this *breaking point, at the very limit of the reading act*.

Stitched into this citation, like so many suturing points which appear to tie together the meaning are those un/translatable French phrases. In the process of signifying signification, the signifier's stuffing or garnishing of the signified, the matter of signification's reflexive enunciation, and the very figure of reading itself, the phrases in question resist unequivocal meaning or sense, thereby presenting us with what might be called a knotty problem. *Difficult to read, read awry, not read at all*, they confront reading and its impossibility, so that even as we read, we read *what is at stake*, and, simultaneously come to comprehend *that we are in the register of analytic discourse*.

All at once, this is so easy and so difficult to read. Lacan, with that customary, breezy diffidence, merely remarks that the *dimension of 'being read' (se lire) suffice[s] to show this*. Yet, how are we to read that reflexive formation of the verb? It reads itself, and yet, from one language to another, we find it both readable and unreadable, *at the very limit of the reading act*. This is not simply a question of translation, in the simple sense of what can be translated, and what remains, from French into English. This partially translatable, partially untranslatable figure which turns itself on itself, and in itself, while suspending meaning in dividing itself through self-reflexion, alerts us to the fact that, for Lacan, the significance of the signifier lies not so much in the fact that it bears meaning, as that it affirms its function as signifier even as it resists being placed in the role of being merely the bearer of meaning. It stuffs, it garnishes itself. More specifically, it comes to do this. It does this repeatedly and, in doing so, draws attention to its own performance even as it defies reading. Thus reading halts. There comes about a lapse in meaning in this, and the other phrases in French, in Lacan's French. While it is possible to read these phrases in *different ways*, it is *precisely for that reason that they are difficult to read, are read awry, or not read at all*.

The question of reflexivity, where the signifier plays with the very meaning it refuses to assign, inscribes the kind of divisive trait of which Peggy Kamuf has spoken. This is, furthermore, not a simple act, taking place once only. Instead, slippage, displacement, disfiguration, and the movement which *analytic discourse* attempts to read while confronting all the time the difficulties of reading, return within every act of signification. We might read this in the very first of the French fragments: *vient truffer*. Translated simply as *stuffs*, it would perhaps be better to translate this as *comes to stuff.* The verb *venir*, which has been muted in the English, its movement and enunciation silenced in favour of a simple present tense, enunciates occurrence, movement, arrival, development. There is motion, a matter of temporality also. *Difficult to read*, *vient* nonetheless slips within itself, from itself, while enunciating, we would argue an iterable temporality, a movement of constant coming to be, so that what we are given to read in this expression is that *while something is produced by way of meaning* or as if signified, nothing is signified so much as the slippage or disfiguration which brings reading to a halt, causing it to *go awry*, and yet which speaks of reading to-come. The signifier comes to stuff the signified. In doing so, it makes it(self) difficult to read, it comes to be not read at all, while, in slipping, enunciates (in itself) *in other words* in a manner akin to what Emmanuel Levinas calls *an inexhaustible surplus*.

The reading processes that we have just seen at work suggest, first, that the statement commented on exceeds what it originally wants to say; that what it is capable of saying goes beyond what it wants to say; that it contains more than it contains; that perhaps an inexhaustible surplus of meaning remains locked in the syntactic structures of the sentence, in its word-groups, its actual words, phonemes and letters, in all this materiality of the saying which is potentially signifying all the time. Exegesis would come to free, in these signs, a bewitched significance that smoulders beneath the characters or coils up in all this literature of letters.

Emmanuel Levinas, *Beyond the Verse:*
Talmudic Readings and Lectures (1994, 109)

It is neither simply a matter of formal or figural polyvalence, however, nor the pursuance of that in an equally formalised reading gesture. Recognising the *inexhaustible surplus* in *all this materiality of saying* does not come down simply to a matter of discerning what is hidden in sentence structures, grammar, *words, phonemes and letters*, as part of a purely semantic or linguistic register. Were it only that, reading would have begun a thematisation, or, possibly, a *neutralisation*, and, with this, the reduction of the Saying to the Said. We would have been guilty in such an act of reading of abandoning the possibility of *guilty reading* in favour of playing what Emmanuel Levinas calls, with some caution, a 'sign game'.[49]

While Levinas starts repeatedly with *reading processes* and *exegesis* of some textual form, narrowly conceived as a book, a poem, an essay, the Talmud, there is, nonetheless, an other purpose at work in the process of reading. This is its responsibility, for Levinas. Reading, in its ethical response, unveils a process of Saying incommensurate with, and irreducible to, the form of what is Said. While, specifically, Levinas is commenting in the ruin above on that kind of interpretation called *Midrash*, the acknowledgement of the Saying which *exceeds*, which *goes beyond*, which *contains more*, than the Said is central to a Levinasian ethics.[50] The ethical moment in reading arrives in the recognition that reading is a response to the Saying of the Other. The *chance* taken in reading is that, in such a recognition, the Saying will fall into the Said.

At the same time, however, running the risk of domesticating the Saying, at the *very limit of the reading act*, there comes the chance of perceiving through the movement of difference how *it is the **Saying** that always opens up a passage from the Same to the Other, where there is as yet nothing in common ... there is both relation and rupture, and thus awakening ... An awakening signifying a responsibility for the other.*[51] In the chance that reading takes, assuming it to be attentive, patient, trying persistently to find the right speed, the right rhythm, and resisting itself the fall into that purely thematic habituation, there arrives this comprehension of non-simultaneous *relation and rupture*. Reading opens to itself the already opened minimal dislocation or *very slight discrepancy* which is termed by Levinas an *incompressible non-simultaneity*.

Thus reading proceeds, and is possible, as we know, via the undecidability and irreducibility of difference. The motion of reading as process is remarked structurally in the first sentence of the citation, and remarked by Levinas in the announcement of a *first* movement: *the statement commented on exceeds what it originally wants to say.* This commentary, this reading, does not rest here, however. It continues, even as it exceeds and extends itself: *what it is capable of saying goes beyond what it wants to say.* There is partially readable the figure of an *incompressible non-simultaneity*,

This latter clause reiterates and moves beyond that reading which precedes it. It thus reads the reading, even while the former commentary remarks in anticipation what will come to be remarked in the following clause. Adumbration *and* accretion; *relation and rupture*. Then, the next analysis: *it contains more than it contains*. Reading is illustrated in its own action. Reading makes this possible, even as it pushes up against its very limits.

We read, for example, that there is a statement. In commenting on that statement which is elsewhere commented on, Levinas reads in this instance, not the statement but the act of reading. We read that the statement says something other than what it wants to say. This something other belongs, not simultaneously but in the disjointing time of reading, to the statement and to the reading. That this something other, this saying, is articulated within the said of the statement, and yet is not fully articulated,   *not yet*   that it is immanent, is acknowledged in the phrase *it is capable of saying,*   *this reading is still not yet what it already is*   and in the reading of that capability as that which *exceeds*, that which *goes beyond*. Beyond this, and yet, still within the *statement commented on*, in what is perhaps the most enigmatic of the expressions concerning reading and saying, Levinas identifies that *it contains more than it contains*. Last of the three readings, this comment returns us to the idea of the statement, before the desire to speak is exceeded, before the potential to speak has extended beyond the desire to articulate.

Exceeds. Goes Beyond. Contains more. Each figures differently, and yet in a readable relationship which is not reducible to absolute similarity or simple repetition, that *inexhaustible surplus of meaning   potentially signifying all the time*   what that is, is not rendered as the said of the explanation. In tracing this structure, therefore, we have opened to us, our reading opens onto this opening, the *discrepancy* or *dislocation* of which Levinas speaks, elsewhere   *a very slight discrepancy, but wide enough for the discourse of skepticism to creep into it without being choked off by the contradiction between what its Said means and the meaning of the very fact of uttering a **Said**.*

A dislocation which, though minimal, would be wide enough to swallow up skeptical discourse, but without stifling itself in the contradiction between what is signified by its Said and what is signified by the very fact of articulating a Said   the rhythm of Levinas's writing–reading in the first sentence of the fragment above announces and performs the encounter with *all this materiality of the saying.*

All the same, 'autodidacticism' does not imply that you can learn nothing from others. Only that you learn nothing from them unless they themselves learn to unlearn. The course of philosophy is not propagated in the way a body of knowledge is transmitted. It is not done by acquisition.

This is clear in the case of philosophical reading, which makes up a large part of the dialogue we have with ourselves on a particular 'subject'. This reading is philosophical, not because the texts being read are philosophical – they could just as easily be by artists, scholars, or politicians. And you can read texts without philosophizing. Reading is only philosophical when it is autodidactic, when it is an exercise in discomposure in relation to the text, an exercise in patience. The long course of philosophical reading is not just learning what has to be read, it is learning that reading is never finished, that you can only commence, and that you have not read what you have read. Reading is an exercise in listening.

Forming in yourself this capacity for listening in reading is forming yourself in reverse; it is losing your proper form. It is reexamining what is presupposed or taken as read in the text and in the reading of the text.

Jean–François Lyotard, *The Postmodern Explained* (1992, 101)

If Saying is in part apprehended through beginning to read the movement of an *inexhaustible surplus*, and freed in the act of reading,   *incipit*   responding to this Saying requires, all the more necessarily, a vigilant, and patient, act of *listening. Reading is an exercise in listening.* Reading listens.

This is one possible definition of reading, one answer, if you listen, to the question *what is it to read?* The answer comes back, not in the formula 'reading is listening', but, instead, as 'reading listens'. The former implies substitution and equivalence. 'Is' operates as a translator, effecting passage and providing a path, smoothly from one to the other, as though the two words were the same. 'Is' installs the sign of equivalence, like two parallel railroad tracks, the purpose being to get from *a* to *b* with our selves intact, transported and yet the same.

Reading listens, however. That's another matter. This answer suggests, barely perceptibly, what reading can do. A feature of reading is made visible, without the formulaic reduction of reading to another term, as though listening were all that reading was, as though the term 'reading' were somehow insufficient and needed support, prosthesis, replacement. *Reading listens*: this hints at a patience, an attentiveness, as the precursor to the response which it already is. Perhaps we can go so far as to suggest that reading begins by listening, in listening. Listening gives up the self,   *I escape myself, I uproot myself*   giving it over to the *chance* reception of the articulation of the other. This is, in part, reading's *incipit*.

To reiterate: reading listens, therefore. It is read as an auditory response to the constant Saying. Or, rather, it can be. In listening to the endless whisper   *inexhaustible surplus*   reading must keep itself open to what, in turn, it appears to open, what it frees, and which, in turn again, it must give ear with ever greater attention. There is a responsibility in reading-listening which, before responsibility returns as the response of a reading-writing, needs to acknowledge that there is no proper time for reading. Reading can never keep up with itself, but is, it must be understood, always already dislocated. It is opened within itself and to itself, between, for example, the Saying of the Other and the reading-listening or, then again, between a reading-listening and a reading-writing. (In reading-writing there is always that possibility that we have stopped listening; or, rather, sign of an *autodidacticism*, one begins to listen to one's self though from some other place within which is never quite the self.)

Not, of course, that these are simply identifiable as positions, or even identities, all at once discrete, self-enclosing, or marked by a *desire for simplicity, for the simplicity we associate with our selves.* For, in the response that is listening, the act of writing is already underway. Similarly, but marked by that *incompressible non-simultaneity*, writing hurries to catch up with

what it always either lags behind, or, otherwise, speeds ahead of in anticipation. From such disabling anachrony we come to hear the following:
*reading is never finished   you only commence   you have not read what
you have read*

To understand this requires that the reader must listen with ever greater
attentiveness. Reading must not listen indiscriminately, but only with an
ear open just wide enough,   *tightly articulated*   open, let us say, to
detail.[52] Open to everything, we understand nothing; we read nothing, we
never begin to read. Neither stopping our ears,   *resistance to theory
reading-towards-socialism*   nor leaving them totally open (which is
not to be receptive, merely passive), we must discompose ourselves
by seeking to control the opening of the reading ear, so as to make reading possible. This is, in one sense, what it is, to read   *an exercise
in patience*   which is to give oneself over   *losing your proper
form*   to the knowledge that *reading is never finished.*

As if to make this point more forcefully, our beginning-reading of the
passage by Jean-François Lyotard returns to us, in other words, a remark
concerning reading, already announced, as an inaugural gesture. (Can you
hear it? Have you heard it already?) In this, we find ourselves returning
also, to where we had believed we had begun, to the sense of *philosophical
reading*, of reading *as philosophers*, and, guiltily, to the reiteration of the
question *what is it to read?* It is this we hear again, and to which we must
not stop listening,   *by posing every guilty reading the very question that
unmasks its innocence, the mere question of its innocence*   as a sign of that
exercise in patience, which is also an *exercise in listening.*

Such an endless exercise, always returning, marks for Lyotard   *endless foreword*   the motion of reading without limits, reading as the
erasure of limits. Reading figures and, in the process, opens onto that *escape*
from *simplicity* of the *self*   *losing your proper form*   in order to
efface the judgement, that which, you will recall from Peggy Kamuf's
fragment, and which returns here, is *presupposed. Philosophical* or *guilty*
reading is heard in this, perhaps. It is in such exercise, of *patience*, of *listening*,
that one discerns the constant effort to proceed by *chance*, so as to avoid
prejudgements or *presuppositions*, or to 'take as read' the very idea that
nothing could be simpler than reading.

Can you hear this phrase?   *taken as read in the text and in the reading
of the text*   can you hear what the phrase appears to be saying? Take
that commonplace expression, *taken as read*. The suggestion is that reading
is done, over with, that we no longer have to concern ourselves with
reading. Reading is *taken as read* and, therefore, no longer need be pursued.
No longer should – need – we listen. But listen further, pay attention to
the way in which Lyotard extends this phrase, doubling its reading and its

implications, internally. *Taken as read in the text and in the reading of the text.* There is heard here that which is not read, which, supposedly, is comprehended   *presupposed*   ahead of encountering the text. And there is also that which is *taken as read* in the act of reading, so that, in appearing to read, reading is policed, cordoned off, prevented from straying from the *path*.

Yet, what we cannot 'take as read' is that the act of reading must not limit itself in its response, and that listening as one form for that response entails hearing the enunciation *that reading is never finished*

By 'the ethics of reading' ... I mean that aspect of the act of reading in which there is a response to the text that is both necessitated, in the sense that it is a response to an irresistible demand, and free, in the sense that I must take responsibility for my responsibility and for the further effects ... of my acts of reading.

J. Hillis Miller, *The Ethics of Reading: Kant, de Man, Eliot, Trollope, James, and Benjamin* (1987, 43)

This fragment of J. Hillis Miller's clarifies why *reading is never finished.* The act of reading comes as a response for which the reader must take responsibility. Responsibility does not end with this response, however. There is not a simple structure, a resolvable teleology of cause and effect, where on one side there is the text, simple and complete, on the other, the reading of that text, equally as simple. The matter of reading does not simply come to a halt, and the idea that the duration, however extended, could one day call a halt to its own act by coming to an end, is mistaken.

For even as the act of reading takes place, it places itself in the position of making itself available to other acts of reading, issuing its own *irresistible demand*, while also being haunted by that demand, issued to which the act of reading is the response, for which it is responsible. There is a doubling, a ghostly disturbance. In this, is the effect of reading. Thus, the reader must also take responsibility for the effects of reading to-come.

Reading must be measured to that extent that responsibility is not only situated in and by the response, but that it must take responsibility for the future conditions of reading's reception which are, strictly speaking, *incalculable*   *the reading in question has already entered the circle of the text, already become an immanent moment of its movement*   reading's responsibility is, therefore, in the *inexhaustible surplus* which reading not only responds to, but which it also puts into play. Acknowledging that it is capable of maintaining that indefatigability, even while it must seek to negotiate without bringing under control the undecidable; is this not a recognition of how reading sets foot into *the circle of the text*, how it has already been anticipated in this gesture? And is not this recognition the first step in a response which, in understanding itself, takes responsibility, as Miller puts it, for its responsibility, or which, in the words of Althusser, *takes the responsibility for its crime as a 'justified' crime?*

Therefore, our praxis is not only a reading of texts but a reading *between* texts.

What does it mean to read between the texts? In a certain sense we always read, when we read, 'between' (the lines for example), because reading always involves a space of presentation where the figures gesture to each other in configurations and constellations that present more than any single figure means. But the structure of the space between the figures, which is determined by them and determines them, is shaped in more particular ways than by the mere universal differential relation of all signs.

Rainer Nägele, *Echoes of Translation:*
Reading Between Texts (1997, 13)

Nägele's commentary opens itself to the space of reading. It requires that we read between its lines, extracting from it its secret   *an ineluctable secondary*   yet, this secret is already on display, in the open. For the passage, in directing its readers to that space between, wherein reading always takes place, enacts the condition of its own commentary   *For even before reading reproduces the sense of absolute knowing, whether affirmatively or **ex negativo**, through its supplementary interpretive addition to the text, the reading in question has already entered the circle of the text, already become the immanent moment of its movement …*

In opening the question of reading through the insertion of that figure *between,   deferred reciprocity*   a figure which, in a certain sense, is already installed in the structure spoken of by the critic, the act of writing on reading displaces   *rhetorical displacement*   its initial constative act. The constative act promised is that of the anticipated critical reading of reading, of *reading-between*. Between you and I, between Rainer Nägele and the reader, every reader, between the critic and whichever text he or she opens. The critical gesture, which is always supposedly a commentary upon something, all the while maintaining its distance – the question of the constative is the question of spacing *par excellence* – immediately doubts its efficacy, in opening itself, unfolding itself, turning its innards outwards.

There is a double operation at work here, *an experience that does not stop at the breaking point but outlasts it*. The question, uttered from the space of critical consideration, can be read as emerging from within that consideration, as the doubt which gives the rhythm of reading pause. Coming from both within and without, moving into the text, and emerging from it, this question, of what it means to read between the texts, unfolds the resonant structure of Nägele's prop- osition   *This is what one has to read and at the same time what one cannot read. From the moment reading is part of what is read, from the moment the divide holding them apart is crossed … then all calculations are opened onto the incalculable, that is, onto a certain future*

In this, the constative collapses in upon itself. It places its operation in full view, all the while maintaining the question as question,   *suspend- ing reading*   the secret of reading-between still to be   *always-yet- to-come*   uncovered. It then proceeds to perform for us. Nägele's rhetorical definition enacts the structural performance it claims to define. There is a great deal of instability here. Figures gesture, like actors on a stage. Yet they gesture in both configurations and constellations. This is what words, do, in being read. They dance, they resonate. They perform. They shed light. Their performance assumes different, differing shapes. On the one hand, the figures assume their promised destiny in enacting a configuration, the reading of which we determine. On the other, the figures assume the stellar mapping of a constellation. Even as we read this, we pull the strings of these marionette-like figures, drawing them into the shapes which we seek out, between the words, between the texts.

There is slippage here, inevitably and ineluctably. For Rainer Nägele, having begun with the constative assertion, a definition or a reading if you will, of an activity, that of reading, slides almost imperceptibly from the reader to the read. This occurs in the act of reading itself. From the constative definition of a praxis, to the performative enactment of language. 'We' begin by reading, we end in the acknowledgement of the seemingly semi-autonomous staging which language, specifically written language, plays out for our entertainment, our sense of enquiry   *we can discover in a text only what we ourselves are but were unaware of*   how can this be, how can there be this paradox? Moreover, how can the paradox be more than double?

Reading always involves a space of presentation. Theatricality itself. We read what interests us, or we attempt to, even though *we can discover in a text only what we ourselves are but were unaware of*   *not everyone carries out the act of reading in the same way*   we insert ourselves, as reading beings, assuming this role, into the between. This is the very condition of the *interest*: between being, or being between. This space between, determined and determining, the articulated location and locution of the figures emerges through reading, allowing reading within writing   *one must be able to stay nimble as one reflects, and stay on the 'surface' whilst reading between the lines*   reading activates the anticipation of the recognition of the structurality of structure, and not merely a universal or idealised sense of structure. No, for in every recognition there occurs the actualisation of the spacing, as the performative spacing occurs, as the critic puts it in particular ways.

Thus we enter this passage, as we would the corridor of a building, and, looking around, find ourselves in the middle of a perform-ance,   *almost impossible to bring under control   losing your proper form*   in the *theatre* of the text. And the performance had been waiting for us all along. For what it means to read between texts is that we respond in the role of the reader to which we are assigned. We acknowledge through our performance our textual location and the dislocation of our selves, and, thereby, admit also our *responsibility* not only for our role, but the acts of reading which result as the effect of our response

*where text is elaborated as **theatre** and as **reading***

But the same goes

But the same goes for all commentary, on any author, on any text whatsoever. In a writer's text, and in a commentator's text (which every text in turn is, more or less), what counts, what thinks (at the very limit of thought, if necessary), is what does not completely lend itself to univocality or, for that matter, to plurivocality, but strains against the burden of meaning and throws it off balance. Bataille never stops exposing this. Alongside all the themes he deals with, through all the questions he debates, 'Bataille' is *nothing but* a protest against the signification of his own discourse. If one wishes to read him, and if this reading rebels right away against the commentary that it is and against the *comprehension* that it must be, then one must read in each line the work or the play of a writing *against* meaning.

This has nothing to do with nonsense or with the absurd ... It is – paradoxically – a manner of weighing, in the very sentence, in the very words and syntax ... a manner of weighing on meaning itself, on given and recognizable meaning ... And reading in turn must remain weighty, hampered, and, without ceasing to decode, must stay just this side of decoding. Such a reading remains caught in the odd materiality of language. It attunes itself to the singular communication carried on not just by meaning but by language itself, or, rather, to a communication that is only the communication of language itself, without abstracting any meaning, in a fragile, repeated suspension of meaning. True reading advances unknowing, it is always an unjustifiable cut in the supposed continuum of meaning that opens a book. It must lose its way in this breach.

This reading – which is first of all *reading* itself, all reading, inevitably given over to the sudden, flashing, slipping movement of a writing that precedes it and that it will rejoin only by reinscribing it elsewhere and otherwise, by ex-scribing it outside itself – this reading does not yet comment. This is a *beginning* reading, an *incipit* that is always begun again.

Jean-Luc Nancy, *The Birth to Presence* (1993, 336–7)

for all commentary, on any author, on any text whatsoever.

This should seem familiar by now, though its reiteration is nonetheless necessary for having the appearance of a recapitulation, of sorts. Both statements, the one concerning reading on the part of Jean-Luc Nancy, the other the apology for necessity, appear to assume a reiterative condition. Indeed, Nancy's opening remark, *but the same goes for all commentary, on any author, on any text whatsoever*, encourages and even cajoles the reader into heading in this direction. It is perhaps as a means of **beginning** *reading*, that an *incipit* is remarked, as the sign that there is in reading that which *is always begun again*. The semblance of familiarity, and of structures of return – consider the commentary on *chance*, above – or, to put this another way, the assembly of resemblance, takes the *weight* off reading, allowing us to stop listening. This occurs in favour of a more idle gaze, indiscriminate and lacking focus. Moreover, semblance as re-semblance also takes the *weight* off both response and responsibility   *the difficult chance*   it is precisely in constituting the likeness that we attempt to close the circle, return to the path, create a frame in which we install the re(as)semblance and, in the process, block our ears.

If we rush to the assumption, if we *presuppose*, that the fragment of Nancy's text is, simply,   *desire for simplicity*   a recapitulation (putting, as it were, the head back on the textual body, in order to finish off the family likeness, and thereby inter reading), we come face to face with two related questions: why does reading have a greater, though more difficult, *chance* of proceeding in the dark, through the blindness of listening, through the understanding of auditory response as reading? And why does the gaze somehow limit reading or blind us to it?[53] Reading must begin by returning, by turning back, and by proceeding in the dark as it attends to the Saying of the Other   *true reading advances unknowing* and this, then, is its *chance*   *simply the effort and the fatigue of the difficult chance*   and, as Nancy lets us know, this is the ineluctable motion of *all* **reading.**

Significantly, what we are given to read here, in order to begin over again, is the careful negotiation between singularity and generality. This is indicated by Nancy through the reference to Bataille as author and the text which is signed in the name of "Bataille", and remarked as such through Nancy's use of quotation marks. (Which, of course, mark off the name from its other inscription, directing us to read the difference between those two uses of the proper name.)

Bataille provides for Nancy the singular example, but, at the same time, this name signs a general textuality addressed in passing as *all the themes he deals with, ... all the questions he debates.* The general condition of the exemplary and singular text implied in the name *Bataille* (which at one and the same time countersigns itself, in that it names both a *writer's* and a *commentator's text*, and *does not*, therefore, *lend itself to univocality*) is described, albeit fleetingly for this instance,   *inevitably given over to the sudden, flashing, slipping movement of a writing that precedes it*   as the gesture of an *incipit*. It is this displacement which Nancy invites us to read. This opening is caught, as is the tension, the spacing between one text and another, between generality and singularity, on the one hand, in Nancy's commentary on that *all* that Bataille's text addresses, and, on the other, in the insistence that *one must read in each line* that which 'Bataille' resists in his own discourse. *All* and *each* thereby figure the movement between generality and singularity which disfigures and thus displaces from within any possibility of *univocality*.

The passage remarks, then, even as it performs its effect through its own passage, the general condition of reading, or, rather, the conditions to which all reading should aspire. This is the case whether one is speaking of the discussion of Bataille, or on the fragment in general. The regulations by which reading takes its *chance* – and even in this commentary there is the inscription of balance and counter-measure, *chance* and regulation, the signs of weighing, by which reading is set, or sets itself, in motion – are commented on clearly in three places.

First: it is acknowledged how *any text, every text*, is a *commentator's text*, to greater or lesser extents. Every writer is a commentator, an analyst, a reader, and every reader also writes or analyses in some measure. The reciprocity at work here is not a sign of simple equivalence, of symmetry, but is, rather, the opening of a necessary and inescapable diachrony – which is also an anachrony – if reading is to take place, to have its *chance*. This is understood if we understand how every writer is his or her own reader, and how every reader, in beginning the act of reading, engages in a process of writing. Thus the figure described here is not so much circular, as it is a somewhat risky movement of return, a turning back as well as an effect of revenance, a haunting. In this turn and return, there is also that passage, in reading's taking effect, of *the sudden, flashing, slipping movement of a writing that precedes it and that it will rejoin only by reinscribing it elsewhere and otherwise, by ex-scribing it outside itself.*

Second: however provisional or intimate an act, reading always remains spaced, placed and displaced (displacing itself in being reading) *just this side* of its act of analysis. In maintaining the act of what Nancy terms *decoding*, reading, prior to any abstraction or articulation of meaning – which term names the suspension of reading – strives towards its own limit. However, *all* reading, even that reading which pushes *at the very limit* through its *unjustifiable* incision into the body of the text, is always inescapably enmeshed in the movement of language. Or, we should say, simply, language, because there can be no comprehension of language, of its motions, its rhythms, without an awareness of articulation – that is to say, the passage of *communication* (however fraught, exhausting, or impossible this may be).

Third (and here we return to a point made in the first remark concerning the general condition of reading, as well as finding the return of a point made elsewhere): all reading slips into a writing, which has already begun, of course, as the a priori gesture on which reading is predicated, of necessity. This is not simply a moment of absolute origin, however. For reading returns, even as writing returns through reading.

So we read therefore, in the commentary on reading's generality, through attention to the singular effects by which reading proceeds and, indirectly via the detour or singular example of Bataille *contra* 'Bataille', how Nancy *sets the text to work*. Erasing any identification of reading and writing as univocal or static oppositions, and resisting falling into the production of a meaning which suspends reading, Nancy *weighs* the means by which reading and its impossibility proceed. Through this, we begin to read the *weight* of responsibility imposed by the general condition of reading, and not only as a general condition but also in every singular act of reading. Reading announces itself as *a manner of weighing* without hurrying to decide on a meaning. The responsibility of this *manner of weighing* serves in turn as a possible counterbalance to the *guilt* of that *unjustifiable cut*, by which reading, *all* reading, must begin.

And, as we know, *the same goes for all commentary, on any author, on any text whatsoever.*

Reading. No doubt this will be the shortest section of the essay, if I ever get to it. In this part I intend to perform a reading of *Celui qui ne m'accompagnait pas*. This is the essay I have promised, and which originally I intended to write ... without referring to another single text. ... Furthermore, I also acknowledge now and throughout this essay, that having to take care of the three preceding sections first is a kind of avoidance of this last bit, that is to say of the real matter at hand. Avoidance is resistance in polite company. Usually this taking care of the commentary is just considered to be the necessary condition of something called scholarship, but I invite all to consider the possibility that scholarship can be a more or less polite name for *reading avoidance* (which does not presume that we know what *reading*, without the *avoidance*, is). I invite my readers to consider the possibility that my attempt is the very symptom of the anxiety of avoidance.

Thomas Pepper, *Singularities: Extremes of Theory in the Twentieth Century* (1997, 175)

I invite my readers to consider that my attempt is the very symptom of the anxiety of avoidance. There is about this statement something of the *structure of confessions and denials of desire.* Guilty reading comes face to face with the very strategies by which the desire to read encounters its own difficulties, and, in doing so, hides its guilt only to compound it, by side-stepping reading's *irresistible demand* and its incalculability.

What we are presented with is a hypothesis concerning what passes for the act of reading, or, at the very least, the preliminary gestures by which prevarication or *avoidance* motion in the direction of a reading, while setting in motion a form of *idling.* That which Thomas Pepper reads in the structure of *avoidance* is that which precisely has gone unread, and which no doubt remains so, in the name of convention, or what is named here as *scholarship.*

This is not to say that scholarship does not read. It is, however, to begin to read scholarship otherwise. It is to position oneself so as to inaugurate a reading between the lines of what can become traced as the effects of scholarship. It is to read in the structures which a certain approach to scholarship puts in place, the construction of limits which, in turn, produce an analytic lapse into non-reading   *whereby the prior principle is simply augmented, its rationality smoothly developed*   and so on. This, we might say, is *taken as read.*

Reading avoidance is one possible name for the reading of what is *taken as read* and which goes unread. Being polite, giving a polite name – such as *scholarship* – to the *avoidance* of reading, signals a sense of embarrassment in the matter of reading. Confronting that embarrassment is to begin reading.

However, there is a very real concern here. In all our efforts to ensure we read, and as we approach reading so as *avoid* slipping into what Pepper calls *reading avoidance,* there is the undeniable manifestation of anxiety. Striving to be responsible to the *irresistible demands* which reading imposes, thereby multiplying all the symptoms of our anxiety, there is always the *chance* that we will *avoid* the incalculable *chance* of reading. There is always, for example, the temptation to return to the protocols of *scholarship* as a means of calming that anxiety, as the citation acknowledges. We are forced to concede a double-bind, with which our acts of reading are inescapably complicit.

Why should this be so? Doubtless, it is in the face of the incalculable, and when confronted by *infectious reading,* that we start to come down with the symptoms. How could it be otherwise? Although *not everyone carries out the act of reading in the same way,* nonetheless there is that commonality   *the same goes for all commentary, on any author, on any text whatsoever*   of *infection* exposed by the symptom of anxiety, and made manifest in all those careful, cautious gestures, those preliminary remarks, which proliferate, and none of which, it has to be admitted, can stop the spread of reading's contagion.

Avoidance might thus name an allergic reaction in the face of an unstoppable difference whereby **writing** *has no sooner begun*

Writing has no sooner begun than it inseminates itself with another reading.

Jean-Michel Rabaté, 'Lapsus ex machina' (1984, 79)

than it inseminates itself with another reading.

This has been implied, of course: repeatedly and insistently, the force, the rhythm of insistence building with repetition, as a cumulative effect, perhaps the effect of reading, or the gathering signs of contamination. There has also been the insistence throughout that reading is a form of writing, that the former always moves in the direction of the latter, the one translating itself into the other. Reading carries in it the traces of a writing, a prior inscription as well as an inscription to come, incalculable in its effects.

Yet we need to avoid even the hint of an apparently linear formulation, and not simply as one more cautious circumscription concerning reading, manifesting in and through its trace the double symptom of *anxiety* and *avoidance*.

Hence this fragment, which folds the reading–writing movement back on itself, while unfolding another gesture: a writing–reading. This figure is not a simple inversion or reversal, but rather a disarrangement which announces a certain temporality, and the matter of spacing also, by which reading proceeds. The indication is one of a writing inseminating in itself a reading,   *not yet what it already is*   which is not an immanent reading which will be present at some moment, where reading, having flowered into meaning, comes to rest, as though reading were only this momentary bloom, a coming to fruition. Instead, the reading inseminated in the act of writing is the figure which remarks the doubling action of beginning *again*, and, in tracing this, gestures towards a reading *always-yet-to-come*.

If for no other reason than this, we must risk acknowledging a distinction between different understandings, of what it means to read.

Reading ... must not claim to reveal hidden meaning, to translate the text into its proper, literal language of meaning; reading must pose itself as an act which sets the text to work, as a work which deconstructs textual oppositions to testify to figural differences.

Bill Readings, *Introducing Lyotard: Art and Politics* (1991, 52)

This remark has been anticipated everywhere, though nowhere as such, always in other words. We – or, at least, I – should have seen it coming. It dares to define, with an apparently breathless gesture, and deceptive simplicity, two incommensurable forms of reading. Or, put this another way, the differing claims for reading around which this essay has turned, to which it has returned.

While *avoidance* is the sign of a resistance to reading, and perhaps also a *resistance to theory* in particular contexts, there is also that necessary *avoidance* of the manner of reading against which Bill Readings first cautions us. Thus, we can read in that definition of the reading which claims to *reveal hidden meaning*, or to render the text *into its proper, literal language of meaning*, the signs of what Thomas Pepper names *scholarship*.

What challenges such a reading which is always a reading-towards-conclusion is the idea of another reading, reading as *act*, and as that which *activates* the text, *which sets it to work*. Such an act of reading would have to begin, perhaps, by attempting to read how those *readings which are determinate with respect to their meanings* proceed, how they operate through attempting to control the limits to which reading can go. Such an act would take responsibility by acknowledging how *the reading is part of what is read*, and, thereby position, once again, the question

> *what is it to read?*

[T]eaching (how to read) remains elusive and blinding as it remains the promise of future illumination. But it is a future that will never have completed its task in the present. There was, for the one for whom I-write, a history consisting of many scenes of pedagogy. In fact, you learned far too many lessons. There was still never enough time to read. On the streets, in the schools, reading. Piano lessons, cosmetics, reading. The runs in your stockings, Hegel, reading. B-ball, concert tickets, reading. This opens the dossier of another scene of finitude's score, the place of a reading that starts from scratch, or from a metaleptic scream, and from the silence of one who, refusing to respond, still dwells in language. The figure of the inscribing/cry, the *Schreiben/Schrei*, the *cri/écrit*, continues to haunt these pages.

Avital Ronell, *Finitude's Score: Essays for the End of the Millennium* (1994, 6–7)

Nearing the end of this essay, these thirty plus circumambulations around the question of reading, we are forced to admit that we are still no nearer an answer to the question: *what is it to read?* We remain close to it, our closeness an immeasurable proximity, which names the intimacy   *just this side*   figured by the *close* in the expression *close reading.* That figure, of being close, also sounds what will never happen to reading: its close, its completion.

But every determinate addressee, and thus every act of reading, is affected by the same 'death,' it therefore follows that every countersignature has to wait on others, indefinitely, that reading has no end, but is always to-come as work of the other (and never of the Other) − a text never comes to rest in a unity or meaning finally revealed or discovered. This work must also be a work of mourning. In truth, only this situation allows a text to have a 'life' or, as we shall say later, an 'afterlife.' For the moment, let us hang on to the fact that the written text presupposes this mortality of empirical writers and readers; it is therefore indifferent to their real death: to this extent the text is inhuman … and in its very principle exceeds the resources of any humanist analysis.[54]

We keep reading close, even though it gets away from us. We know that we will never have done with it, that we are unable to catch up with (what we read as) reading's promise, and knowing also that, after our deaths, there will still be reading to-come. *The act of close reading* speaks of an on-going performance, intimate and yet frustrated, frustrating in its irreducible propinquity. *On the streets, in the schools, reading.* We might say that we are in its neighbourhood.

Understanding this matter of proximal spacing, which all reading re-introduces, gives one to comprehend how, in one's relation to the other, there can be neither homogeneity nor amalgamation. Despite the desire for unity which drives a certain reading, and the self's attempt to read after this fashion, all reading   *but the same goes for all commentary*   only serves to bring the reader face to face with the experience of alterity, of difference and discontinuity.

In coming to terms with the question of the vicinity   *on the streets, in the schools*   of reading and, at the same time, the impossibility of ever being at home with reading, we hear one possible answer, articulated by Avital Ronell, in response to the question, *what is it to read?* Reading, and, as importantly, *teaching (how to read) remains elusive and blinding as it remains the promise of future illumination.* This is the case whether we consider this *future illumination* as, on the one hand, the *incalculable*, while, on the other hand, *the sense of absolute knowing.*

We might wish to ignore that promise, if only in order to calm things down a little, to keep something in place for a while. We might rush to read this fragment as merely a biographical narrative, the order of which

is a little skewed (doubtless, a 'literary' effect, and, therefore, to be discounted, not read, or never read as such[55]). The initial impression thus
received from this extract is one of a disjointed linear temporality, linearity
available despite the effect of displacement, through that kind of a reading
that reassembles and simplifies. Flowing from the future promise of
reading to a past concerned constantly with learning to read, desiring to
read, there is discernible a single narrative.

This is the very reading which we are enjoined to avoid by Bill
Readings, the kind of reading that translates the text into its meaning.
Such a reading produces a unity from the trajectory of the life, the I who
writes. To produce a life in this fashion would be to reduce the text to a
state of unreadability, closing it off from its future reception, from that
future that will never have completed its task in the present. The closeness, the
intimacy of the reading that is put in process here would be closed were I
to present a reading of the kind which reduces the effects of the figural to
the biographical meaning. Such proximity, articulated in part by desire,
would be closed to itself also, unavailable to Ronell for the analysis of
reading. There would be no reading without a spacing and an incom-
pletion, without figural displacement and substitution, which the translation into a meaningful unity would cancel or otherwise downplay as
merely 'literary' effect.

The writing self thus opens itself in its attempts to read and thereby
remains close to its other. In the act of inscription, reading is announced
even as it remains fraught with difficulties. Reading may well be
escape   *escape in broad daylight*   but it also escapes. There is never
time for reading, never the right time, *never enough time to read.* It signals
that which is left but *remains* the promise of future illumination. Reading
remains elusive even as it countersigns the remnant as the elusive *remains*
which escape, again and again, insistently   *reading has no end, but is
always to-come as work of the other   its temporality is that of an always-yet-
to-come*   this is announced everywhere in the figural performativity of
this passage, in its temporal passages. In this, the text is not simply either
readable or unreadable. Rather it pushes at the limits of the reading act,
negotiating between the promise of a reading and the fact that it cannot
be read. It folds and unfolds itself, onto itself where *reading is part of what
is read.* There is remarked in this citation of Ronell's text the *strange time*
of reading, of that which precedes and that which is *not yet   necessarily
still to come*   as we will come to understand, shortly, on turning the
page, and, in so doing, find that we have turned back, that this question of
reading's impossible time has returned to us.

For the moment, however, notice the figural rhythm in this fragment.
Notice how it enacts the condition of the promise, how it precedes our

attempt at reading while, through the iterable pulse, it displaces itself within and from itself. Although there is *never enough time to read*, or, perhaps, precisely because of this lack whereby all our efforts are mis-timed, reading is everywhere, while the task is never completed. Reading (dis)figures any simple temporal narrative or biographical delineation, displacing, disjointing through a manifest, serial iteration, from which the very question of the *readable is indissociable.* The performative and the analytical modes and motifs cannot be separated. Reading returns to haunt this passage, to disrupt its flow, as a figure to be read. As the haunting, iterable inscription belonging to both past and future, hidden and presented in the partial reading of a life, reading behaves as though it were the sign of metalepsis itself, as though in its serial returns it traced the movement of metonymic substitution of rhetorical figures, one after another. Announcing itself four times, taking place hurriedly, reading arrives too late and yet to come. Each figure of reading figures this impossible, unbearable situation. Every utterance of *reading* countersigns itself as metaleptic figure, supplement and displacement, of every other figure of *reading.* There is no origin for reading, no absolute starting point to which we can justifiably point. It is the work of the figure of reading that allows us to read this. In working in this way reading opens *the place of a reading*, while maintaining in this opening the proximity by which the hope of reading must proceed.

However, while there is *never enough time to read*, reading's meta-leptic act, its performative disturbance of any simple descriptive function   *that is what one has to read and at the same time that is what one cannot read*   and its affirmation of itself as never itself, does not refer merely to those obvious figures of reading. Reading, as figural effect, allows us to attend to the way in which the I-writing speaks of its history as *scenes of pedagogy*, through the metalepsis at work through all those figures, each substituting for every other. *Hegel. Piano lessons. Concert tickets. On the streets, in the schools.* These and each of the other instances of this history are the figures which the inscribing/cry of reading puts to work as metonymic substitutions, one after another, one for another as the places of reading and as *that which remains to be read.* To this extent, Ronell's remarks, substituting the pasts and futures of reading as disfigured iterations of one another, suspend, as Peggy Kamuf puts it, *the trait of reading* **in** *the text and* **of** *the text.* We are thereby brought face to face with one of the conditions of reading and its impossibility, which is that

The unreadable is fixed only to the extent that it is apprehended as that which remains to be read, even if that reading is theorised (as it is in Derrida's work) as belonging as much to an immemorial past as to the future. An example of this would be the piece of graffiti quoted by Derrida in 'Border Lines': ' "do not read me" ' [Derrida 1979, 145]. This injunction must and cannot be read. ... This piece of graffiti concisely illustrates the double-bind of deconstruction, in other words the necessity and impossibility of deconstructive reading. It demands and dissolves the strange time, which is never proper, never *on* time, of reading. The reading of this injunction not to read can never catch up with itself, can never coincide with itself, not least because it can never have adequate authority to authorise its own reading ... and because its very readability cannot be derived: what is readable is indissociable from what is iterable. The readable has no origin, it is immemorial, it precedes us and our reading. By the same token the readable would be necessarily still to come. It is still to come not as an act or event that might one day become present, but rather in the structural sense of a promise, a promise which is – in its affirmation and nonfulfilment – a double-bind.

Nicholas Royle, *After Derrida* (1995, 161–2)

the unreadable is fixed only to the extent that it is apprehended as that which remains to be read, even if that reading is theorised (as it is in Derrida's work) as belonging as much to an immemorial past as to the future. Nicholas Royle's argument concerning the unreadable is partly readable in, and as an effect of, that fragment of Ronell's. The citation is unreadable to the extent that it enfolds the time of reading, and the idea of reading as always to come into its own passage. Arriving after the event, as readers, we read that, in a certain past, reading was never caught up with, that it always returned, and that reading remains to come, in a future which will never be present. Reading *precedes*; it is *necessarily still to come*. As we have seen, the passage plays on the troping of biographical figures so as to embed the difficulties of reading and thereby enact its *strange time, which is never proper, never on time*. It might be said then, that Ronell's text provides an exemplary performative instance of Royle's statement on reading's time and the deconstruction of a linear temporality.

Furthermore, and with respect to singularity, the matter of reading's time, of what takes time and mistiming, is already remarked in other words, in part, in the ruins of the texts of Hamacher, Kamuf, Ronell, amongst others. In acknowledging this, I am already too late. Too late in commenting on this, it is already too late to comment on Royle's passage also. It is too late to suppose that this ruin can be cited at this juncture as though it somehow confirmed all that had preceded it, as though this were an authoritative statement towards which this essay had been heading. (Although, it has to be admitted, this fragment does seem to operate in this manner.)

The question of the temporal ruin of reading, of reading's own ruined temporality and what such dilapidation entails is clearly articulated here. Moreover, this passage is already ruined, not only in its own mediation with the time of reading but also in its dispersal and anticipation, in this essay. It is, for example, broken up into fragments of itself, elsewhere, in certain annotations for example, though not restricted to this (n. 24, 26, 37). There is in this the effort to enact the double-bind in the structuring of this essay, whereby what precedes and what is still to come is announced indirectly, through acts of spacing and displacing, within and as a condition of reading. Such a procedure constitutes a necessary response and, within that, an acknowledgement of what has to be read and what, at the same time, cannot be read. This book has proceeded in part by chance, but also by a strategy of supplementary disjointing, or disturbance within, and as part of its own frame. Such fragmentation forces reading to confront its own limits, suspending reading, and turning it towards its own unreadability.

Recall Hans-Jost Frey: *The fragment is unreadable: it has not been read when one takes notice of what is there nor can one read more than what is there. The fragment is fragmentary because it says less than it should. Something is not there, and this lack must be read as well. This is why it is not possible to talk about the fragment without also talking about what is not there.*

Responding to nothing other than fragments, we have sought to navigate their various commentaries on reading and, simultaneously, come to terms with their lack, so as to set the texts to work, rather than reducing them to a meaning. In seeking to obey the injunctions concerning reading by which the fragments are structured, we have, nevertheless, transgressed the law of reading affirmed by each of these texts   *the reading of this injunction not to read can never catch up with itself, can never coincide with itself, not least because it can never have adequate authority to authorise its own reading*   in so doing, we have, of course, been faithful (though never absolutely) to the impossible conditions which reading puts in place as that which it displaces within itself.

Thus, the authority supposedly conferred by the citation is already displaced throughout. This is, after a fashion, what is at work in the passage by Royle, where Derrida is cited, or where, to be more accurate, Derrida is cited aphoristically, citing an aphoristic instance of graffiti (described by Iain Sinclair as *polaroid epiphanies*[56]). The fragment fragments, it ruins even as it seems to authorise: for Royle's source is ultimately anonymous. (As such, and in its anonymity, *it can never have adequate authority to authorise its own reading*, even though, it is precisely over the question of the authority, the law, that this remark is cited.) The citation of Derrida is merely an expression of resonant re-citation, fragment within a fragment, employed by Derrida to confirm the textual *double-bind*.

Read a little more of Derrida, from the same place: *All these texts, it should now be clear, involve law and transgression, and the order that is **given**, and the sort of order that can be obeyed only by transgressing it beforehand. Read yesterday, among some graffiti: 'do not read me.' I continually ask what **must** be done or not be done (for example in reading, writing, teaching, and so on) to find out what the place of that which takes place, is constructed upon (for example the university, the boundaries between departments, between one discourse and another, and so on).*

Recognising the structural necessity of the *double-bind* allows us to begin to read differently, to displace the idea of reading from within and thereby displace ourselves as readers. Consider, for example, the differential relation within any structure   *what counts, what thinks (at the very limit of thought, if necessary), is what does not completely lend itself to univocality or, for that matter, to plurivocality, but strains against the burden of meaning and throws it off balance*   as it is articulated in the following expressions: *law and transgression, affirmation and nonfulfilment, necessity and impossibility.*

These name in particular ways what the question of reading must confront, what reading can be said to come down to, time and again, without being reduced to a fundamental principle or an original articulation. The phrases in question do not operate as pairings of discrete identities or separable unities, reliant on an either/or logic. Rather they remark economically the mutual determination and reliance of the one on the other, without simple priority. While these phrases might be read as emphasising certain spatial differences within texts, they also indicate the temporal problematic that is intimately entwined in reading. This structure is played out in a different manner in the abyssal reduplication indicated above: Royle citing Derrida citing an inscription without provenance.[57] And every time the graffito is re-presented, the *double-bind* of reading returns with undiminished force (even though *it can never have adequate authority to authorise its own reading*).

Consider Peggy Kamuf's commentary on the same injunction:[58] *That negative imperative phrase enacts, in the most economical fashion, the predicament of a double bind. The reader is already at fault before the law, before the law which comes **before** or **already**: by reading the command, he or she ignores it; but ignoring the command (by not reading it) does not rectify things, does not equal obedience to a command that also demands to be read, that is, to be acknowledged as command in order to have the force of a command. Thus, the 'someone who reads' is but the stage of a certain performance positioned by this double bind. That performance is always, in one way or another, to be compared to the act of reading a dictionary entry for **reader**: before one can receive the order of the concept, one has already given an example of it. The predicament is temporal ... because the meaning of the act (its concept) is not given in the present of the performance, it is not one with or immanent to the act, but divides that 'moment' upon itself, disperses it among the non-present modes of before and after the act. The reader reads before the law that he or she comes after. Neither the singularity of an act nor the generality of a concept of reading or meaning can be thought of as absolutely prior to the other, as a cause or condition of possibility of the other. Or rather, both are at once conditions of the other. On the one hand, the order of the concept requires the very act of reading that it defines and defies; on the other hand, the reading act will have been already determined by the order of the concept. Rather than a logical order of determining priority, this relation is one of an irreducible difference, that is, a relation that cannot be comprised by one or the other of the terms. Each moment or term is only insofar as it **is related** to the other. Each moment or term is cut across, divided by the other. Each inscribes the other in itself and is inscribed by the other outside of itself.*

Irreducible difference is remarked by Royle in the acknowledgement of the *past* and *future* of reading. It is also inscribed in that announcement of that which *must and cannot be read*, in that which *demands and dissolves*, and, as we have suggested, in that which both *precedes* and is *necessarily still to come   affirmation and nonfulfilment   here is the problem of reading with which we have to contend, repeatedly, as perhaps *one of the strongest models of a presumed disjunction*

Perhaps one of the strongest models of a presumed disjunction between everyday life and art, stream of consciousness and self-consciousness, is presented in the invisible social space of reading and writing, a space defined temporally and spatially as outside and above the quotidian. Although reading may give form to time, it does not count in time; it leaves no trace; its product is invisible. The marks in the margins of the page are the marks of writing, not the marks of reading. Since the moment of Augustine's reading silently to himself, reading has inhabited the scenes of solitude: the attic, the beach, the commuter train, scenes whose profound loneliness arise only because of their proximity to a tumultuous life which remains outside their peripheries. The reader speaks only to the absent writer; the writer speaks only to the absent reader.

Susan Stewart, *On Longing: Narratives of the Miniature, the Gigantic, the Souvenir, the Collection* (1993, 14)

The *irreducible difference* of, between, the *past* and *future* of reading, its continuous *affirmation and nonfulfilment* with which we have to grapple, announces in the rhythm of reading *one of the strongest models of a presumed disjunction*.

Disjunction marks every reading act. It cannot help this, as *reading transforms the reader and the text at the same time.* The element of disjunction is also read in the constant, necessary return to reading, *to what is impossible for us.* It is signed, furthermore, and countersigns itself, in the seemingly paradoxical movement of reading, where it *is still not yet what it already is.* For all these reasons, and for many others, *reading is a rather risky business whose outcome and full consequences can never be known in advance.* We might even go as far as to suggest that the *resistance to theory* occurs as a recurring fear of that *disjunction* of the self which reading imposes on us; we find ourselves *riven* in and by reading.

There is another aspect of reading which divides us: its *solitude*. Reading causes us to be disjoined from our selves. The supposed unity of the self comes into question. Moreover, in reading we erase our presence, escaping into the text, *escaping in broad daylight* as Hélène Cixous maintains. This is the case whether we read in private, on our own, or in full view of others. While reading has undoubtedly *inhabited the scenes of solitude*, at least since Samuel Pepys,   *the scene of writing and of reading is, like the grave, a private place*   and probably since St Augustine also,[59] as Susan Stewart suggests, it has hidden the reader in plain view,   *we're no longer there*   in what Stewart describes as *the invisible social space of reading and writing*.

Everything about reading intimates invisibility, not least the act itself. The *product* of reading is *invisible*, as is its *trace* (by the acknowledgement of which we begin to discern an abyssal structure). Writing only serves to re-enforce the spacing between reading and writing, reader and writer. Reading returns this opening, though in a different manner. The figures of the *absent writer* and the *absent reader* caught in a process of frustrating communication inscribes what Timothy Clark describes (in citing Derrida and thereby reduplicating the abyssal disfiguration) as *the space 'of deferred reciprocity between reading and writing'.*

With invisibility comes silence and *profound loneliness*. This latter effect of reading is all the more pronounced when reading takes place in the *social space* wherein the invisible reader exists, in *solitude*. The depth, the profundity of *solitude*, which acts of reading engender is amplified when the scene of reading inhabits, if not the same space, then one of nearly unbearable *proximity* to the social. In this description, Stewart's exploration of the condition of reading unfolds a complex, intimate spatial structure wherein reading takes place, even as it displaces the self. While Cixous has identified in such *solitude* a freedom and excitement   *eating the forbidden fruit, making forbidden love*   Stewart's analysis of the space of reading tends towards an unresolvable melancholy.

That reading can cause one to feel both *guilty pleasure* and *loneliness* should not surprise us. *Solitude*, like reading, is neither one nor the other, necessarily. Yet, it is inescapably traced by the memories of both, and the infinite potential for the return of such effects. Neither are discrete, and, as we know, both are capable of slipping into the mode of the other. Indeed, *solitude, loneliness* is itself not simply either pleasurable or melancholy. Capable of both resonances, it requires the patience of a reading turning back upon itself. Furthermore, there is in that melancholy produced by *solitude* a pleasure peculiar to the feeling, while pleasure is equally apt to slide into melancholy of a quite different kind (if only in anticipation of the eventual loss of *guilty pleasure*, or the return of the memory of such pleasure in moments of solitude).

Solitude as *pleasure* is available as soon as we open the book, as soon as we step out of the world. Yet we leave off reading and are consigned to a sense of melancholy which drives our desire to return to the act of reading. All the time we are reading, we know that the *loneliness* of reading becomes another kind of *solitude*, when we call a halt to reading. There is that *absence*, already at work in close reading, and yet there is also the *absence* anticipated in reading, of the moment when we will no longer read, or desire to read. For every time we close the book, put it down, abandon it, we have – even if we do not recognise it or ignore it – the intimation of a future where there is no reading. And this is all the more pronounced when we realise that we have returned to that *tumultuous life*, wherein we feel all the more lonely, all the more melancholy, because we no longer strive after the intimacy of close reading.

Submerged in the *tumultuous life*, we find reading reduced to the blink of an eye, the briefest of responses. In the face of this, our melancholy grows. However, as if to ward off that uncontrollable oscillation within ourselves between *pleasure* and sadness   *scenes of solitude*   and as if to avoid the sense *of time, of chronology, of repetition*, we slip into reading *at a glance*.

By order of experience, one speaks of time, of chronology, of repetition. But some architects are suspicious of time and would wish their buildings to be read at a glance, like billboards.
Bernard Tschumi, *Architecture and Disjunction* (1994, 161)

Reading *at a glance* is hardly reading at all. We now know this. It's as if our
ears were stopped but our eyes were wide open, the lids taped apart, so
that reading could not pace itself, marking its time in the rhythm of
blinking. Such reading, if we can even call it that, hurtles violently, in the
apparent immediacy which strives to erase from the condition of reading
all possible temporal delay. There is an acknowledged brutality in the
glance. It takes less time than *a sort of intellectual journalism*. For all that,
however, we cannot overlook the *glance*, we cannot allow it to slip from
our sight, nor for our attention to slip. We have to teach ourselves to read
the *glance* differently.

   Despite the intended speed–reading which advertising poster designers
have in mind, billboards (amongst other things, graffiti for example) can
be subjected to more rigorous readings, as we have known since at least
either 1957 or 1972.[60] (And here we are, again. Dates as countersignatures,
hinting at moments when a different kind of reading was undertaken. But
to return to the question of reading *at a glance* and billboards.) We can take
time to read, if we choose. Or, to be more accurate, and to recall the point
made in a number of places,   *reading may give form to time*   and
not least implicitly in Bernard Tschumi's fragment,   *the exposition or
operation of reading takes time*   reading takes time.[61] In this, reading also
involves itself, it evolves, as a chronological structure, which is not simply
linear but operates necessarily through *repetition*. This element alone
would make plain the structurality of reading, its spacing, its archi-
tectonics. Yet if *some architects* and, we would argue, some readers are
suspicious *of time, of chronology, of repetition*, this is because they desire
celerity in reading. They embrace speed, if not immediacy, as the limiting
and controlling factor in a reading reduced to less than the blink of an eye.

   According to a conventional or commonplace logic, such a reading is
really more of an appropriation, a consumption in which act every reader
is reduced to a *consumer*, a *user*. Of course, this is what the designer of
the billboard wants, like *some architects*. Immediacy, rather than decoding,
response reduced to acceptance. Or perhaps the desire is for the instantaneity of a deciphering which functions by assuming that, because all
can be seen at once, there is no need to expose the content to the time of
reading, to the chronology which an analysis constructs in the careful
tracing and repetition of the text.

   Such a desire is no doubt engendered by the wish to have done with
critical reading altogether. The *glance* suggests this: look, look away, as
simple as that. However, it has to be insisted that, even in the event of
being confronted by the billboard, the building, the photograph, or that
which apparently places everything in plain sight, in full view, reading still
takes place, and takes time, however brief. The immediacy of content does

not provide an alternative to the spatial or temporal requirements of reading. The question is not reducible to one of *either* immediacy *or* spacing. One cannot read the two terms as opposites.

To see them in this way would be to subject them merely to that mode of reading defined in that phrase, *at a glance.* The very idea of immediacy can only be read if the time is given to a reading which dismantles the distinction between the one and the other, and one thereby comes to an understanding of the time, however brief, which the allegedly immediate reading takes. Moreover, in learning how to reorient our reading in the face of the immediate,   *strains against the burden of meaning and throws it off balance*   we have to comprehend how the time of reading and the spacing which it opens are all the more necessary when confronted by the wish to *read at a glance.*

In order to begin a reading which hampers the rapidity inimical to the act of close analysis, we want to suggest that to *read at a glance* is still not the same as not-reading, even though, in haste, such a reading may be said to assume certain characteristics of not reading. Earlier, we had said, too hastily no doubt, that the *glance* suggests this: look, look away, as simple as that. Of course, it is not this simple; there is still a chronology of the *glance*, which we have been at pains to articulate. The *glance* as reading operates by illumination and allusion, different, differing modes by which reading proceeds. The barest contact, the *glance* nonetheless conveys albeit obliquely. Pay attention to speed, slow it down. Read, so as to mediate against acceleration, but do so within the movement of the *glance.* The *glance*   *how violent reading can be*   is where we slip in and out of reading, it is where reading slips away, but also where we can escape into reading, even as, in the winking of an eye, reading escapes.

This might seem like exaggeration to some, but

This paradox of truth-in-exaggeration also enables us to throw new light on the notion of interpretation. Paul de Man concludes his Preface to *The Rhetoric of Romanticism* with a very concise and far-reaching thesis: 'Reading as disfiguration, to the very extent that it resists historicism, turns out to be historically more reliable than the products of historical archeology.' [de Man 1984, 123] Interpretation is thus conceived as a violent act of disfiguring the interpreted text; paradoxically, this disfiguration supposedly comes much closer to the 'truth' of the interpreted text than its historicist contextualization. How?

Let us focus on Lacan's great readings of classical literary and philosophical texts ... These readings clearly represent a case of violent appropriation, irrespective of philological rules, sometimes anachronistic, often 'factually incorrect', displacing the work from its proper hermeneutic context; yet this very violent gesture brings about a breathtaking 'effect of truth', a shattering new insight ... The key point here is how this 'effect of truth' is strictly co-dependent with the violent gesture of 'anachronistic' appropriation: the only way to uncover the truth of Plato or Kant is to read them as 'our contemporaries' ...

[A]t this precise point, the opposition between 'for us' (the mere subjectivity of the external interpretative gesture) and the 'in-itself' (of the work's true content) is suspended, since the very violent gesture of subjective intervention ... brings us closer to the work In-Itself than any objective historicist approach.

Slavoj Žižek, *The Plague of Fantasies* (1997, 95–6)

this paradox of truth-in-exaggeration also enables us to throw new light on the notion of interpretation.

It would be all too easy to reject the idea that reading can be violent. Indeed, to describe reading as a violent act might be said to be, itself, the expression of a certain violence. At the same time, it could be argued that, in explaining reading through recourse to the figure of violence, one diminishes, or otherwise does not take seriously, the very real forms of violence, physical, personal, political, material, which exist. In such propositions, all of which, to some degree, involve *risk*, there is discernible the effects of reading *at a glance.*

Without wishing to lessen the violence of violence, of what might be termed 'real' violence, it has to be conceded that there are different forms of violence. While no one would deny that an act of reading does not cause distress or pain in anything like the manner of a physical attack, nevertheless, to say we know unequivocally what violence is, and that reading cannot be of this order, is itself a violent articulation. In any statement which seeks to enforce the unequivocal, and that rules out of order the opening of a critical questioning which would consider the ways in which a concept or philosopheme operates, there is an undeniable force, which is all the more unfair, unjust, inconsiderate, and perhaps even brutal in its brevity and arrogance for its being articulated in so totalising a fashion. Such a remark resists absolutely any dialogue, any appeal, any self-reflection or opening of itself. It claims for itself an exaggerated truth, which neither sees the power invested in its exaggeration nor, indeed, comprehends the extremity of its aggrandisement upon which its truth is reliant. The remark that decides on that which is or is not violent, is violent to the extent that it does not consider, and refuses to consider what is meant by violence within the discursive and conceptual framework of its own articulation. To suggest, for example, and as we have already implied, that 'violence is X' or 'violence is not X' is to miss the extent to which the figure or the very idea of violence in discourse or language, before any physical act, is normalised, naturalised, and has passed into an unthought framework within which our subjectivity is constructed.

In thinking in this manner, or rather in resisting or avoiding the process of analysis   *a philosophical reading*   reading is effaced, silenced. For the normalisation of a concept or figure effectively makes mute the responsibility which ethical acts of reading carry, through the tyranny of a common-sense logic, a crude pragmatic sensibility which says 'we know (don't we) what needs to be read, and what doesn't need to be read'. This is to say that we know what reading is, and therefore to have done with the question, once again, which asks, *what is it to read?* So, to turn back on ourselves, to argue that 'violence is X' or 'violence is not X' is simultaneously to avoid reading, to proscribe further reading, and to proceed as though there were such a thing as an *innocent reading*. It is only the *innocent reading* which can claim with a kind of bullying equanimity that it is the only measure of what constitutes the idea of the violent. The *guilty reading*, however,   *takes the responsibility for its crime*   exposes the way in which every reading is a *guilty reading* by *posing every guilty reading the very question that unmasks its innocence, the mere question of its innocence:* **what is it to read?** To read reading as an act of violence is, then, to open reading to its own processes while also to turn to the reading or not-reading of violence which exists in any normative statement concerning what implicitly constitutes the instance of violence.

Five times in this fragment, Slavoj Žižek describes reading as a violent act, a gesture of appropriation and disfiguration. Indeed, the violence of reading is defined through the identification of its features: disfiguration, appropriation, disregard, displacement, factual error, anachrony, intervention. Drawing on Paul de Man and using as his example the readings of Jacques Lacan, Žižek catalogues the powerful effects of critical interpretation. That such effects are powerful may be understood through the *truth-in-exaggeration* which such phrases express, in themselves and through their cumulative operation.

Exaggeration derives from the idea of piling up or accumulation, whether literally or figuratively. In this extract, Žižek's rhetorical ploy is to heap up the figures of interpretive violence. This ploy is all the more forceful for that insistent reiteration of violence, which, while serving to define analysis of a certain kind, also remarks on itself performatively. At these moments, and as a result of the way in which they may be read as suturing the text, punctuating it while also weaving it together, the textually reiterated violence of the interpretation of violence suspends *the opposition between 'for us'* — in this case, Žižek's *breathtaking* analysis of analysis — and the *'in-itself'*, that is to say, the *truth* of an interpretive process, an act of reading, such as that defined by Paul de Man, and carried out, though not represented here, in *Lacan's great readings of classical literary and philosophical texts*.

The suspension of the *opposition* in question allows us to come closer in our acts of close reading, while keeping us   *just this side of decoding*   at the slightest remove, by which opening reading remains to-come. Furthermore, it effectively opens our ears to the limits of reading, while also alerting us to the fact that we can never finish reading. The return to reading, which Žižek terms *'anachronistic' appropriation*, and which he illustrates through allusion to the interpretation of *Plato or Kant* as *'our contemporaries'*, signals abruptly and yet indirectly, how reading *affirmation and nonfulfilment*   survives; its temporality   *a future that will never have completed its task in the present*   is that of an always-yet-to-come. While this comprehension of the critical act is, itself, undoubtedly violent, it nevertheless is open to the reading of violence, and the violence of reading, in a way that *historicist contextualiz-ation   politicising it means culturalising it ... culturalising it means historicising it, historicising it means interring it*   is not (and this, despite the greater violence to which historicisation is prone, as Geoffrey Bennington reminds us). Thus, we might conclude, and as a reminder to ourselves to remain open to reading, it is through understanding the suspension of the *opposition between 'for us'* and the *in-itself* that we may begin to come face to face with the fact that *there is no such thing as an innocent reading.*

Indeed, *we must say what reading we are guilty of*

Notes

Preface and Acknowledgements

1. The discussion which follows is drawn from *The New Shorter Oxford English Dictionary on Historical Principles*, 4th edn, ed. Lesley Brown (1993).
2. On the matter of temporality, and its relation to reading and reading's im/possibility, see notes 26 and 37 to 'Constructions, Citations, Fragments, *Remaniements*', below, and, of course, discussion elsewhere throughout the essay.
3. Derrida has written on the condition and effects of citation in a number of places, but perhaps the most sustained and theoretically informed account of citation is Claudette Sartiliot's (1993), which includes an essay on Derrida's consideration of citation in general, and his performative use of citation in *Glas* (34–73).
4. The citation is taken from the edition of the play found in *William Shakespeare: The Complete Works*, ed. Stanley Wells, Gary Taylor, et al. (1988).
5. On the relation between telepathy, reading, and literature, on the reading mind and 'mind reading', see Nicholas Royle, *Telepathy and Literature: Essays on the Reading Mind* (1991).

Constructions, Citations, Fragments, *Remaniements*

1. Robert Young begins *White Mythologies: Writing History and the West* with the following statement: 'If so-called "so-called poststructuralism" is the product of a single historical moment, then that moment is probably not May 1968 but rather the Algerian War of Independence – no doubt itself both a symptom and a product' (1990, 1).

   And there, I've failed already, promising myself that there would be no notes to this, but instead, being guilty of the act, making too nervous a start. A double start, and more than this: for there is a redoubling here, an excessive multiplication, in re-marking the double moment, which is also that of another, read in another's text, as a doubling which is read as already being doubled, ahead of me, in the acknowledgement of both symptom *and* product.

2. For a different reading of 'strong reading' and its enactment, see Geoffrey Bennington, 'X' (1996, 4–5).

3. The first clause of this statement is one possible answer to a question put by Roland Barthes as the title of an essay: 'Where to Begin?' (1990, 79–91). It also echoes that made by Geoffrey Bennington – 'We must begin somewhere, but there is no absolutely justified beginning' (1993, 15) – which, in beginning the third division of his 'Derridabase', is not so much a beginning as it is a reiteration of remarks made by Jacques Derrida, first in *Of Grammatology*,

> The first gesture of this departure and this deconstruction, although subject to a certain historical necessity, cannot be given methodological or logical intraobitary assurances … The opening of the question, the departure from the closure of a self-evidence, the putting into doubt of a system of oppositions … these errant questions are not absolute beginnings in every way, they allow themselves to be effectively reached, on one entire surface, by this description which is also a criticism. We must begin *wherever we are* and the thought of the trace which cannot take the scent into account, has already taught us that it was impossible to justify a point of departure absolutely. *Wherever we are*: in a text where we already believe ourselves to be. (1976, 162)

Then in *Margins of Philosophy*,

> For the same reason there is nowhere to *begin* to trace the sheaf or the graphics of *différance*. For what is put into question is precisely the quest for a rightful beginning, an absolute point of departure, a principal responsibility. The problematic of writing is opened by putting into question the value *arkhe*. What I will propose here will not be elaborated simply as a philosophical discourse, operating according to principles, postulates, axioms or definitions, and proceeding along the discursive lines of a linear order of reasons. In the delineation of *différance* everything is strategic and adventurous. Strategic because no transcendent truth present outside the field of writing can govern theologically the totality of the field. Adventurous because this strategy is not a simple strategy in the sense that strategy orients tactics according to a final goal, a *telos* or theme of domination, a mastery and ultimate reappropriation of the development of the field. Finally, a strategy without finality, what might be called blind tactics, or empirical wandering … (1982, 6–7)

These statements, which reject the 'absolutely justified beginning', might be read as directing the operation of the present text. Certainly, they gesture towards an excuse for the organisation of the various citations, gathered as so many interruptions or returns. For, given the impossibility of justifying one beginning over another, the textual fragments are ordered alphabetically, according to the proper names, the surnames, of the critics and philosophers, from whose texts these citations have been taken.

Furthermore, the second clause of the remark acknowledges another remark of Derrida's concerning citation: 'Everything "begins" then, with citation, in the creases {*faux plis*} of a certain veil …' (*Dissemination*, 1981, 316). There is here a recognition of the impossibility of an absolute beginning, while performing an operation on the text so as to open its inner workings to our view.

4. As a comment on the technical foreclosure on reading, see, for example, Suhail Malik's comment on technics in general:

> From Aristotle up to – and perhaps including – Heidegger, technics has been taken to be a means to an end … technics as a means isn't just a concrete instrument or thing like a weapon or tool. It can be some rules, a procedure or method for conducting an exercise or ourselves …, or it can be some 'know how', a knowledge or (acquired) skill, which is employed in order to obtain what is required. (1996, 200)

5. Jacques Derrida has commented on the limit to which Althusser's reading of Marx goes, in an interview with Michael Sprinker. It is worth considering Derrida's response, inasmuch as it is instructive concerning the point at which Althusser's reading breaks off, a point of arrest which is markedly similar, from a certain perspective, to that discerned by Althusser in what he might term 'non-philosophical' or 'non-scientific' readings of *Capital*. Derrida's 'reading' here might itself be read as extending the act of 'reading as a philosopher', the 'guilty reading', to the Althusserian reading:

> It seemed to me that according to his reading of Marx, let's say the 'good' Marx is the one who emerges beyond neo-Hegelian metaphysics, beyond anthropology, etc., to finally reach a theoretico-scientific problematic. But I believed and I still believe now that one must pose many historical or 'historial' questions about the idea of theory, about the idea of objectivity. Where does it come from? How is objectivity's value constituted? How is theory's order or authority constituted? … I did not see these genealogical questions, so to speak, on science, objectivity, etc. being posed by the Althusserian discourse, or at least not in a manner that seemed satisfactory to me. From that, it seemed to me that his reading of Marx constituted in dropping a bad text or a pre-Marxist one, let's say, and in constituting the Marxist text … as a text that had moved beyond metaphysical suspicion … good politics never comes from a limitation on questioning or on the demand of thought … I thought that what he was saying was not wrong … but that it was necessary to further question the axiomatic of discourse. ('Politics and Friendship', 1993, 197)

In that moment where necessity for further questioning is raised can be read the question of reading's responsibility, and, implicitly in that, a question of the politics of reading, which extends precisely the Althusserian problematisation of what it means, *to read*

6. On the impossibility of being totally naked, see Jacques Derrida, '"*As if* I Were Dead": An Interview with Jacques Derrida' (1996, 215), which is, itself, a comment on the double reading of nakedness in Yvonne Sherwood, '"White Mythology" or "Metaphor in the Text of Theology": Jacques Derrida among the Prophets of the Hebrew Bible' (1996, 85).

7. It is perhaps possible to read Pepys and Barker as two signatures for the spatial co-ordinates of a certain scene of reading, between the end of the seventeenth century, when this scene assumes a particularly private mode, and the

end – or certainly the latter half – of the twentieth century, when that scene comes to be read for all that it does not appear to say of itself. As the passages by Samuel Pepys suggest, reading is a fraught business. We may perhaps read Pepys as entering on the scene of reading and being disturbed at finding himself in a place not carefully regulated. In short, he does not know how to read what kind of a reader he should become.

Following Pepys' death in 1703, throughout the eighteenth century, there is a proliferation of treatises and discussions of reading, and the role of the reader, as the concern for the performance of the voice is placed in opposition to what Peter de Bolla describes as the ever-present 'counter-force', the text, in the scene of reading (1989, 231). De Bolla provides a fascinating account of the ways in which writers on the 'art' of reading entered into and encouraged efforts to police this scene (1989, 230–78).

8. 'Thence homeward by coach and stopped at Martins my bookseller, where I saw the French book which I did think to have had for my wife to translate, called *L'escholle de Filles*; but when I came to look into it, it is the most bawdy, lewd book that ever I saw, rather worse than *putanta errante* [1584] – so that I was ashamed of reading it; and so away home' (1995, vol. IX, 21–2).

9. 'Thence away to the strand to my bookseller's, and there stayed an hour and bought that idle, roguish book, *L'escholle des Filles*; which I have bought in plain binding (avoiding the buying of it better bound) because I resolve, as soon as I have read it, to burn it, that it may not stand in the list of books, nor among them, to disgrace them if it should be found' (1995, vol. IX, 57–8).

10. 'Up, and at my chamber all the morning and the office, doing business and also reading a little of *L'escolle des Filles*, which is a mighty lewd book, but yet not amiss for a sober man once to read over to inform himself in the villainy of the world. At noon home to dinner, where by appointment Mr. Pelling came, and with him three friends: Wallington that sings the good bass, and one Rogers, and a gentleman, a young man, his name Tempest, who sings very well endeed and understands anything in the world at first sight. After dinner, we into our dining-room and there to singing all the afternoon (by the way, I must remember that Pegg Pen was brought to bed yesterday of a girl; and among other things, if I have not already set it down, that hardly ever was remembered such a season for the smallpox as these last two months have been, people being seen all up and down the streets, newly come out after the smallpox); but though they sang fine things, yet I must confess that I did take no pleasure in it, or very little, because I understood not the words; and with the rests that the words are set, there is no sense nor understanding in them, though they be English – which makes us weary of singing in that manner, it being but a worse sort of instrumental music. We sang till almost night, and drank my good store of wine; and then they parted and I to my chamber, where I did read through *L'escholle des Filles*; a lewd book, but what doth me no wrong to read for information sake (but it did hazer my prick para stand all the while, and una vez to decharger); and after I had done it, I

burned it, that it might not be among my books to my shame; and so at night to supper and then to bed' (1995, vol. IX, 58–9).

11. I am alluding through this phrase to an essay on translation, and a certain question, indirectly pertinent here (between Barker and Pepys, between Pepys and the French/Italian texts of which he speaks), on 'a sexuality of translation' (160) by John P. Leavey, Jr., 'French Kissing: Whose Tongue is it Anyway?' (1999, 149–63).

12. On this kind of descriptive operation as the expression of reading, see Geoffrey Bennington, 'X' (1996, 5).

13. 'To read ... is to make a series of claims for oneself within the contemporary network of social and sexual codes of behaviour' (de Bolla 1989, 236). One might usefully borrow this formula in another context to read the construction of 'Francis Barker' as a reader of Pepys indebted to, constructed by, a reading practice signed in the name of Michel Foucault, or at least as a somewhat *après-Foucauldian* manner. What de Bolla's formulation reveals is that no act of reading is ever entirely private, nor is as easy, as Barker seems to imply, to separate the private from the public, inasmuch as, while reading may occur in private, the reading self is constituted through a network of forces which are neither wholly or solely public or private, social or sexual, and which, through close and patient readings of such figures, could not admit of such separate or separable spheres.

Another interesting comment of de Bolla's is as follows: 'The organisation of society, for example, is reflected in eighteenth-century reading practice in a dramatic and unignorable way: to read is for the most part to indulge in leisure; it is to display wealth and education and to demonstrate the acquisition of knowledge' (234). Despite the 'private' manner in which reading may be carried out, there is a sense, if not in the time of Pepys, then shortly thereafter, that reading has clearly social and cultural ramifications, and is caught up in negotiations with networks of power, which themselves need to be subjected to careful acts of reading.

14. On such gestures in Barthes's work, and his critical resistance to and exposure of 'the ways in which ... [t]he ideological underpinning of social relations ... seek to ground themselves in absolute certainties', see Anthony J. Cascardi's recent discussion (1999, 215–16). Cascardi discusses Barthes's analysis of 'mythical speech', which is, in Cascardi's words, 'a depoliticized form of speech that eliminates contradictions' (216).

Arkady Plotnitsky discusses the passage from Barthes's *S/Z* in his 'Un-*scriptible*' in which we are interested (1997, 243–58). His summary is worth citing:

> *S/Z* begins by establishing the difference between and the hierarchy of the scriptible and the readerly ... At stake is a fundamental evaluation, albeit – and this is important – specific to a certain culture, within which Barthes' discourse operates: each text or encounter with a given work, language, or system is defined by this difference. It may be suggested, more generally, that both the scriptible and the readerly connote in fact, or in effect, situations, economies,

or acts of reading or writing, or, in Derrida's phrase, acts of literature and acts of reading. These concepts refer to engagements (and the impossibility thereof) with texts and, thereby, always to certain *constructions* – or constructions/deconstructions – of texts. (246)

15. On the accusation of 'theory' in the guise of 'deconstruction' as being either too political or not political enough in relation to institutions and politicized discourse both inside and outside the academy, see Peggy Kamuf's scrupulous reading of the situation (1997, 133–61). Richard Beardsworth, considering the text of Jacques Derrida, also provides a telling commentary on deconstruction's account of why 'all political projects fail' (19) as well as its radical assessment of institutions and the violence by which such institutional structures operate (1996, 18–25). See also Geoffrey Bennington's 'Demanding History' (1994, 61–73), 'Not Yet' (1994, 74–87), and 'Outside Story' (1994, 88–98).

16. On the 'aporetic responsibility concerning the political' (68), see Richard Beardsworth, 'The Political Limit of Logic' (1996, 46–97). See also Drucilla Cornell, who comments similarly on the question of undecidability: 'Undecidability in no way alleviates responsibility. The opposite is the case' (1992, 169).

17. Cf. Jacques Derrida ('Afterw.rds …'): 'not only … does deconstruction take on logo-phonocentrism, not only does it question the authority, unity or very identity of the word (the linguistics of the "word", the vocable) but it insists where it is no longer merely a question of deconstructing discourses and semantics, but also and primarily institutional and political structures' (1992, 202).

18. Bhabha resists similar charges of 'liberal pragmatism, academicist pluralism and all the other "-isms" that are freely bandied about by those who take the most severe exception to "Eurocentric" theoretic*ism* (Derrideanism, Lacanianism, poststructuralism …)' in the essay from which the citation above is taken (Bhabha 1994, 20).

19. Bhabha articulates his 'commitment to theory', and to the necessity of reading 'theoretically', through the example of reading John Stuart Mill's *On Liberty* against the grain. The reading, which focuses on passages from ch. 2, 'Of the Liberty of Thought and Discussion' (1991, 20–61), relies on Mill's own acknowledgement on the agonistic and the contradictory within political discourse, or that which makes Mill's reading possible. The difference in reading – the very kind of close reading which Bhabha advocates – is that while Mill imagines the possibility of an eventual homogeneity, resolution, or unity through the agonistic engagement, Bhabha reads the possibility of maintaining the agonistic, so as to read the subject of politics as always already riven, to borrow Francis Barker's definition of the subject. An interesting passage in Mill's text is the following, from which have been borrowed the opening five words:

> It still remains to speak of one of the principal causes which make diversity of opinion advantageous, and will continue to do so until mankind shall have

entered a stage of intellectual advancement which at present seems an incalculable distance. We have hitherto considered only two possibilities: that the received opinion may be false, and some other opinion, consequently, true; or that, the received opinion being true, a conflict with the opposite error is essential to a clear apprehension and deep feeling of its truth. But there is a commoner case than either of these; when the conflicting doctrines, instead of being one true and the other false, share the truth between them; and the nonconforming opinion is needed to supply the remainder of the truth, of which the received doctrine embodies only a part. (1991, 51–2)

While Mill's text seeks to move towards the 'remainder of truth' in some dialectical gesture, what is of interest is that notion of what is shared between apparently oppositional discourses, along with that of the 'nonconforming opinion', both of which suggest the possibility of reading the non-read in a narrowly political discourse. It might be suggested that Mill's is a 'utilitarian' reading, inasmuch as it halts the process of reading at that point where the act of reading has served its purpose. Bhabha's gesture is to extend the process of Mill's reading, thereby making available the critique of Mill's text from the point of its own hiatus, and, in doing so, motioning towards the continuance of reading.

20. Cf. Jacques Derrida, *The Ear of the Other*, 'the texts that I want to read from a deconstructive point of view are texts that I love, with that impulse of identification which is indispensible for reading. They are texts whose future, I think, will not be exhausted for a long time' (1988, 87).

21. Cf. Jacques Derrida, *Right of Inspection*, '[t]he exposition or operation of reading takes time' (1998, 11). Derrida here differentiates between the reading imposed by a purely, narrowly textual form, such as a novel, which is implicitly spatio-temporal in organisation (and disorganisation, for it disorganises the unity of the text as book), and the reading imposed on the gaze by a visual text, such as a photo–novel, of which he is writing, here.

22. The phrase 'from and of the other' is recalled from Derrida's essay 'Che cos'è la poesia?' (1991, 227), where the poem is 'from now on a certain passion of the singular mark, the signature that repeats its dispersion' (235). That 'singular mark' is, I would suggest, provisionally, the 'accent of deviation' which Bloom seeks to read. For a reading of Derrida's essay, its relationship to the text of Heidegger, and the question of the impossibilities of reading, summed up in Bloom's statement that '[e]very reader is an Idiot Questioner. He asks "who wrote my poem?"', see Boris Belay's 'Translating Istrice', in which he asks of the signatures of Heidegger and Derrida: 'How can they ever be mine, how can I ever cite them, make them close to what at heart is me, recite them, know them by heart? How can I ever respond to them, to even one of them? How can I be responsible to them, to do justice to them?' (1999, 166). We might suggest that Belay's question is an antithetical return to Bloom via Heidegger and Derrida, deviating from Bloom's question precisely in its maintenance of the unresolvable problematic. Derrida catches at this problematic elsewhere when he speaks of the risk of translation

(which might be another translation for 'reading', in his 'Letter to a Japanese Friend', when he writes 'When I speak of this writing of the other which will be more beautiful, I clearly understand translation as involving the same risk and chance as the poem. How to translate "poem"? a "poem"? ...' (1991, 276; it is tempting to read the final question, which leaves the essay without closure, promising a future reading, or the futurity of reading, as that which Derrida begins to read, eight years later in 'Che cos'è la poesia?'). Bloom is attempting to 'respond to the call of Poetry', to use Belay's summary comment on Derrida, but whereas Bloom reads all such response as the expression of anxiety, Derrida celebrates the im/possibility of reading, of translation, of responsibility. The text of Heidegger to which Belay specifically situates Derrida's essay is *Poetry, Language, Thought* (1971).

23. Royle, in commenting on hostility towards the text of Derrida in general and the so-called 'Cambridge affair' concerning the award of an honorary degree, has remarked that 'there is not reading and there is not reading' (1995, 160). On what Royle calls, appropriately, this 'farce', see Derrida's own response, in an interview entitled '*Honoris Causa:* "This is *also* extremely funny"' (1995, 399–419).

24. On the unreadable and the undecidable which propels reading, which commands that reading begin again, rather than bringing a halt to reading, see Nicholas Royle, 'On Not Reading: Derrida and Beckett' (1995, 159–74).

25. The citation comes from a commentary of Clark's (1992, 110) on Derrida's essay 'Force and Signification' (1978, 3–30).

26. A number of comments – readings which are also writings – could be added here, but a few will have to do for now. Of the structural impossibility of the authoritative reading, Nicholas Royle has remarked that 'what is readable is indissociable from what is iterable' (1995, 162), the truth of which is borne out in the passage by Timothy Clark, in the passage between Derrida's 'Force and Signification' and Clark's text, and, again, in the passage between both of those and the present text. Royle continues: 'the readable would be necessarily still to come. It is still to come not as an act or event that might one day become present, but rather in the structural sense of a promise, a promise which is – in its affirmation and nonfulfilment – a double bind' (1995, 162). This passage and further commentary on it will return, below.

   Royle provides a significant analysis of the double-bind of reading/ unreadability by Samuel Weber in a note to his own discussion: 'every text ... is both structurally unreadable and yet destined to be read. It is structurally unreadable inasmuch as it can never be definitively delimited or situated (*casé*); it *is* only *as* the repetition of other readings, which in turn are the reinscription of other writings; and hence, the desire to repeat it for once and for all, to read it properly, is inevitably frustrated. And yet at the same time, this desire is unavoidable', Samuel Weber, 'Reading and Writing *Chez* Derrida', *Institution and Interpretation* (1987, 97–8, cit. Royle 1995, 172 n. 8).

Geoffrey Bennington has this to say:

> the fact remains that in order to write I must read myself, if only in a minimal
> sense, in the moment that I write. The act of writing is from the first divided
> by this complicity between writing and reading, which immediately prevents
> one from considering this act so easily as an act, and blurs at the same time
> the activity/passivity ... distinction that underlies the usual understanding of
> writing. (1993, 53–4)

As he puts it elsewhere in the same text, 'it therefore follows that every
countersignature has to wait on others, indefinitely, that reading has no end,
but is always to-come as work of the other ... a text never comes to rest in
a unity or meaning finally revealed' (1993, 56). See also his comments a
couple of pages further on, on the 'power of repetition in alterity' and the
'relation of finite and infinite' (1993, 56–8).

27. On this subject, see n. 15 (and the discussion to which it is appended), in
which the reader is referred to the following remark of Peggy Kamuf's: 'The
fact that deconstruction can be positioned as at once too political and not
political at all, as both PC and not PC, signals the terms in which the political
is posed in this debate are inadequate to account for all the effects being
produced' (Kamuf 1997, 146). There is an immeasurable gap between
Bennington's 'not political enough' and Kamuf's 'not political at all', which
would make for interesting reading, or which would bare careful commentary on the extent to which either 'theory' or 'deconstruction' remains
unread and even unreadable, in conventional political terms, whether from
the 'Left' or the 'Right', whether from a 'Left-Liberalism' or a 'Right-
Liberalism'.

28. Again, see Kamuf's *The Division | of Literature* (1997), particularly ch. 5,
already mentioned. Her following remark is also of interest, in that it
implicitly acknowledges the limits of reading 'theory', and the extent to
which 'theory' has stopped being read:

> If it generally seems to be the case that – to use a very sloppy kind of shorthand
> that the academic institution not only tolerates but prefers and proliferates –
> 'French theory' has been forced back into some kind of retreat from the shores
> of humanities and particularly literature departments in the United States, then
> this retreat has not occurred without leaving behind an offshoot that is usually
> called simply 'theory.' 'French theory,' in other words, may have been put under
> some kind of general ban, but "theory" without the qualifier has won what,
> for the moment at least, seems to be a respected place in catalogues of graduate
> literary studies. (1997, 12)

The sloppiness of 'French theory' has been replaced by the banality of
'theory' as a catch-all identification, and what is interesting also in Kamuf's
astute summation of the situation is that, to an extent, the location of 'theory'
in 'graduate literary studies' suggests an implicit cordoning off of the reading
material of theory, from undergraduates to a large extent. Paul de Man's
resistance to theory is re-marked in precisely this organised, if tacit proscription
of reading within the institution. Following the formula through, not only

are undergraduates not given the opportunity to read 'theory' (if we stay with the general term for the moment, if only for convenience's sake), they are also not encouraged to read in a so-called 'theoretical' fashion. Kamuf's remarks apply specifically to the university in the USA. In Britain, it is possible to find a number of theory courses for undergraduates, although it would require statistical research to show whether these are more frequent in Britain than in North America. What can be said, however, is that, often, 'theory' courses are taught during the last year of undergraduate study. Effectively, this limits the extent to which the student can ask questions concerning what it means to read.

On the question of the institutional reception of 'theory' and the attempted stabilisation of 'theory' singular, see Jacques Derrida, 'Some Statements and Truisms about Neologisms, Newisms, Postisms, Parasitisms, and Other Small Seismisms' (1990, 63–94).

29. The phrase 'nonsynonymous substitutions' is employed by Derrida in the essay 'Différance', in *Margins of Philosophy* (1982, 12).

30. On the institution of literature and literature in the institution, see Kamuf (1997, 3–12). In part, the discussion which follows is indebted to Kamuf's reading of *literature*.

31. Philippe Lacoue-Labarthe 'theorises' the 'figure' in the following way:

> The 'theoretical' consequence (though at the limit of the theorizable): the figure is never *one*. Not only is it the Other, but there is no unity or stability of the figural; the imago has no fixity or proper being. There is no 'proper image' with which to identify totally, no essence of the imaginary. (1989, 175)

Lacoue-Labarthe describes how the figural is marked by a 'destabilizing division', which 'perhaps accounts for the logic of the *double bind*' (175).

32. Simon Critchley offers the following commentary on part of the fragment in question:

> In the Genet column, Derrida finds what he calls 'the good metaphor' for describing his interpretative practice …
> […]
> With this 'good metaphor', we can see that what Derrida is trying to avoid in reading is a relation to mastery over his object, the kind of dominating mastery that Sartre exerted over Genet in his *Saint Genet*, where the object of interpretation is imprisoned within this dialectical and emancipatory narrative of existential psychoanalysis. Rather, Derrida pictures the reader within the cabin of a rather clumsy dredging machine, manipulating a series of levers. A steel mouth scrapes the bottom of the sea with what Derrida calls a 'toothed matrix', picking up morsels here and there, but letting the water and silt pass between its teeth. The operator of the dredging machine can barely hear the sea from within his cabin.
> What this metaphor shows, I think, is that however much the philosophical hermeneut may wish to elevate a particular literary text into an order of meaning or give a coherent interpretation, water and silt will inevitably slip through the teeth of the reading machine and *remain*. … whatever transcendental, metalinguistic or hermeneutic key is employed to unlock the text, such a

matrix will always let the text fall back and remain as a remains. In this sense, we might say that the goal of Derrida's reading practice is to *let the remains remain* (1997, 146).

33. On metaphor and metaphoricity as transport, as movement, see Derrida's 'The *Retrait* of Metaphor' (1978, 1998, 102–29). As the citation from *Glas* places Derrida at the controls of reading's dredging machine, involving him in a process of gathering which he cannot wholly control and which will never be complete because of that which slips away and remains, so in the later essay, Derrida goes further by suggesting that '[w]e are not in metaphor like a pilot in his ship' (1998, 103). Although Derrida seeks the good metaphor for reading, nevertheless, even if he finds it, he will never be able to gain mastery over it, he will never be able to steer it. Metaphor will drift, such is its figurative dimension, and so the reader will be forced to drift with it.

34. This might be summarised in a remark such as: 'We haven't got the time to read in any other way because we need to get to the point where we no longer need to read.'

35. This is not to say, of course, that a feminist reading, or, to use a riskier phrase, a reading-towards-feminism, is always structured by a resistance to reading differently. Nothing could be less true. As Felman makes clear, any act of reading can all too easily fall into a blindness with regard to its own procedures, and thus succumb, in the name of a politics or an agenda, to the unread assertion of its own *ideologies and preconceptions*.

36. I take this phrase from Thomas Pepper, who defines the 'absolute construction' in the following manner: 'In its grammatical usage, an absolute construction is so called because it is independent of its grammatical surroundings. Ablative in Latin, genitive in Greek, the kind of clause to which I refer has something of the unconditioned condition about it' (1997, 89).

I want to suggest that each of the citations found in *Readings* may be read as operating as if they might be absolute constructions, depending on what follows each citation and whether it is modified by it or not. As Pepper puts it, '[i]f what follows modifies [the statement] ... then the phrase is not absolute' (1997, 89–90). However the independence, or otherwise, of any statement is not a simple matter, as Pepper goes on to show, borrowing from Paul de Man, for the question of 'absoluteness' or 'independence' is a matter of positionality; the citation or statement's 'absoluteness, its independence is dependent on what follows or precedes' (1997, 91). The problem here is precisely the problem of reading.

37. The matter of timing and rhythm might be said to be the crucial concern throughout this book, something which, if not discussed directly (as though I could stand apart from matters of rhythm and tempo in relation to reading, while trying to find the right way of writing on that very subject, of 'reading reading' and reading its unreadability), is performed everywhere.

An exemplary comment on this question is provided by Derrida ('The Art of *Mémoires*'), in a footnote, appropriately enough, to a discussion of the movement of interpretation:

> And yet reading must find its rhythm, the right measure and just cadence. In the measure, at least, that it attempts to bring us to grasp a meaning that does not come through understanding. Let us recall the epigraph to *Allegories of Reading*: '"Quand on lit trop vite ou trop doucement on n'entend rien." Pascal.' (When one reads too swiftly or too slowly one understands nothing.) One should never forget the authoritative ellipsis of this warning. But at what speed ought one to have read it? On the very threshold of the book, it might be swiftly overlooked. (1989, 88, n. 3)

The complexities of this annotation are many. It may well remain the unfulfilled task of this essay to read this statement. It is the case, no doubt, of finding the right rhythm. Derrida is referring here to a specific moment of reading. To be precise, he is addressing Paul de Man's interpretation of Baudelaire's modernity, and the question of memory also.

The issue at stake for de Man is one of temporality, and, in particular, the expression of a paradox (quite readable as being akin to the paradox to which we have directed our attention in the citation of Hamacher's text) in Baudelaire's use of the phrase – de Man calls it a formula – 'la représentation du présent' (Baudelaire 1923, 208, cit. de Man 1971, 156; alluded to by Derrida in 'The Art of *Mémoires*' (1989, 60–2)). Baudelaire's 'conception of modernity' (de Man 1971, 156) is caught in this phrase, 'which combines a repetitive with an instantaneous pattern' (156), which, we would argue is readable, albeit expressed in a different manner, throughout the present text. Derrida's reading of movement in de Man's reading is the occasion for the visible installation of a number of frames, structures within and across structures. Reading signals in this instance both structuration and potentially infinite opening or regress.

Of the epigraph from *Allegories of Reading*, Nicholas Royle comments: 'to read this is at once straightforward and impossible. The sentence must and cannot be read at the right speed, according to a proper sense of time' (1995, 161). It is this double bind addressed by Hamacher's text which will also be the focus of the fragment to follow, by Peggy Kamuf.

38. See Heidegger's 'The End of Philosophy and the Task of Thinking' (1993, 431–49). The conclusion of the essay is of interest in relation to Hamacher's discussion:

> In what circle are we moving here, indeed, inevitably?
> Is it the *eukukleos Alētheiē*, well-rounded unconcealment itself, thought as the clearing?
> Does the title for the task of thinking then read, instead of *Being and Time*: Clearing and Presence?
> But where does the clearing come from and how is it given? What speaks in the 'There is/ It gives'?
> The task of thinking would then be the surrender of previous thinking to the determination of the matter for thinking. (1998, 449)

This passage provides the starting point for Luce Irigaray's reading of Heidegger (1999), in which she looks at Heidegger's forgetting of 'air' in his concentration on the figures of 'earth' and 'ground' as constitutive metaphors in the philosopher's critique of metaphysics. In the translated edition of Irigaray's study, the translator, Mary Beth Mader, translates the passage from 'The End of Philosophy and the Task of Thinking', from its French publication, which appeared prior to the German language version. The translation is notably different from the one given above:

> In what circle are we here, and truly with no way out? Is it the *eukukleos aletheie*, the without-withdrawal [*le sans-retrait*], perfect roundness, in its turn thought as *Lichtung*, as the clearing of the opening? But then won't the task of thinking have as its title, instead of *Sein and Zeit*, Being and Time: *Lichtung und Anwesenheit* (Clearing and Presence)? But whence − and how − is there clearing *(gibt es die Lichtung)?* What must we hear in this *there is / it gives (es gibt)?* The task of thinking would then be the abandonment of the thinking in force until now so as to determine the proper matter for thinking. (1999, 1)

In departing from this passage, and, in particular, the *es gibt*, the *there is / it gives*, Irigaray investigates on what ground Heidegger constructs the questioning of metaphysics and how that questioning (not peculiar to Heidegger though, perhaps, more pronounced in his text than elsewhere) is reliant on the unread figure of matter, solidity, foundational material, despite the expressed desire for opening and clearing.

In a certain way, Hamacher's passage involves a fraught negotiation of these same questions, a desire to keep the path, to acknowledge the framing work of structure, but get off the path, and to take the unmappable detour. In this context, as fanciful as it might seem, it might be the case that the *es gibt* can be responded to with the *as it were*. The apparent certainty of the *there is / it gives* waivers before the loosening of structure from within structure that *as it were* effects.

The French translation of *es gibt* is, on a number of occasions, *il y a*. As Mader points out about this phrase, *il* 'is an impersonal pronoun that (allegedly) functions as a purely grammatical subject. In the expression *es gibt*, *es* is a personal pronoun, neuter except when used demonstratively, ... used as a subject of an impersonal verb' (Irigaray 1999, 181 n. 1). Elsewhere, Mader makes a further comment on the phrase *il y a*: *il y a* has an existential sense without using the French verb equivalent of 'to be'; it instead uses the French equivalent 'to have' (186 n. 2). Furthermore, the French not only inscribes impersonal anonymity, it also withdraws the giving of *es gibt*.

The *il y a* is a recurrent interest in the text of Emmanuel Levinas. As Adriaan Peperzak puts it, 'The expression *il y a* translates the German *es gibt* (there is), but it receives a very different interpretation from Heidegger's: rather than the generosity of a radical Giving, *il y a* is the name of a dark and chaotic indeterminacy that precedes all creativity and goodness' (1996, ix). The first essay on this subject was '*Il y a*' which was subsequently incorporated into *De l'existence à l'existant* and first published in 1978 (1994,

29–36). It speaks of a condition prior to – *even before* – being, or, as Levinas puts it in *Ethics and Infinity*, addressing the *il y a*: 'It is something one can also feel when one thinks that even if there were nothing, the fact that "there is" is undeniable. Not that there is this or that; but the very scene of being is open: there is. In the absolute emptiness that one can imagine before creation – there is' (1985, 48). In *Time and the Other*, in answer to the attempt to imagine what he calls 'this existing without existents', Levinas remarks: 'Let us imagine all things, beings and persons, returning to nothingness. What remains after this imaginary destruction of everything is not something, but the fact that there is [*il y a*]' (1987, 46). See also his *Totality and Infinity* (1969).

On Levinas and the *il y a* see Dennis King Keenan, *Death and Responsibility: The 'Work' of Levinas* (1999, 15–18, and throughout). See also Thomas Carl Wall, *Radical Passivity* (1999, 27–30, 70–3, 116–17) and Jill Robbins, *Altered Reading: Levinas and Literature* (1999, 92–9). In the context of reading, Robbins's discussion is particularly useful. As she makes plain, in Levinas's text, art and the *il y a* are 'conceptually linked … This intrication is irreducible … because the seeming necessity for Levinas to employ numerous literary examples and illustrations in his presentation of the *il y a* and because Levinas's very access to the *il y a* is via an aesthetic category, the imagination' (93). At the same time, the *il y a* is 'ungraspable', as Wall puts it (28), it opens, performs, and traces, an 'equivocal interspace', an 'interval between being and nothingness' (Keenan 1999, 16).

Refer also to Derrida's discussion in *Given Time* of the expression *es gibt*, as it relates to the movement of Being in relation to the idea of the gift (1992, 18–23).

39. The doubling figure of fiction which I am imagining here, wherein the closure and the limit are themselves marks of a reopening, is developed from Jean-Luc Nancy's sense of the relationship between finitude and the infinite, and his discussion of the way in which, in that relationship, finitude is never, finally, itself, never, finally, finished or what he calls 'privation' (1997, 29–33).

40. However, as Derek Attridge points out in paraphrasing Derrida from 'Ulysses Gramophone' and 'Aphorism Countertime', 'what we call "chance events" are made possible only by the pre-existence of a network of codes and connections' (Derrida ed. Attridge 1992, 253). That this essay proceeds by chance is only possible inasmuch as the network of citations and fragments is put in place; chance arises as a result of the negotiation between the calculation of remnants and the effort to remain open – to remain *nimble* as Sarah Kofman puts it, below – to chance encounters.

41. In understanding that which reading opens onto, that to which the act itself is open, as, for example, in the *incalculable*, I mean to suggest, following Nancy, that the 'open', and as he puts it, has neither some 'vague quality of an indeterminate yawning nor that of a halo of sentimental generosity. Tightly woven and narrowly articulated, it constitutes the structure of sense qua sense of the world' (1997, 3). Inasmuch as it breaks off, remains unreadable as such, and cannot be read *finally*, the textuality to be read serves

to constitute its own possibility of reading-to-come, and thus articulates both its own opening, and the opening which the act of reading seeks to trace. This does not, however, mean, nor should it be implied, that one can read as one wishes, or that texts can mean anything one wishes, or indeed, that texts mean nothing and can therefore mean anything you choose them to mean. Reading textually, to recall de Man's phrase, means to be aware that the text is open only to the extent that we respond to its own tightly woven constitution.

42. On the aphorism, see Derrida, 'Aphorism Countertime' (1992, 411–33) and 'Fifty-Two Aphorisms for a Foreword' (1989, 67–9). See also Nicholas Royle, 'Philosophy and the Ruins of Deconstruction', in his *After Derrida* (1995, 124–42).

43. The fragment of Kofman's text is drawn from her discussion of Nietzsche's will to misunderstanding, his desire to resist a too facile reading, to which ends he employs aphorism, and what Kofman terms an 'obsessional' or 'metaphorical writing' (1993, 113), which in its strength actively seeks out the appropriate reader.

44. This last sentence should be taken as an aphoristic countersignature to Nicholas Royle's *After Derrida* (1995) which I have cited elsewhere. There is readable here a ruinous citation of Royle.

45. Elsewhere (1986, 74–88), in the essay 'Semiotics: A Critical Science and/or a Critique of Science', Kristeva talks of the literary text as 'practice' and 'productivity', which terms keep in play the sense of process and perform-ance suggested by *theatre* and, less immediately, from certain perspectives, *reading* (but the immediacy is, itself, a question of reading). This essay, and 'Word, Dialogue and Novel', from which the fragment, above, appears, were both published in *Séméiotiké. Recherches pour une sémanalyse* (1969), from which the following commentary on reading comes:

> For the ancients the verb 'to read' had a meaning that is worth recalling and bringing out with a view to an understanding of literary practice. 'To read' was also 'to pick up', 'to pluck', 'to keep a watch on', 'to recognize traces', 'to take', 'to steal'. 'To read' thus denotes an aggressive participation, an active appropriation of the other. 'To write' would be 'to read' become production, industry: writing-reading, paragrammatic activity, would be the aspiration towards a total aggressiveness and participation' (1969 cit. and trans. in 'Ambiviolences' by Stephen Heath, 1984, 31; see n. 49, below).

Kristeva's etymological revivification of the verb 'to read' offers a useful corrective to Barthes's idle and intransitive reader produced institutionally through the readerly text.

46. The proceedings of this conference were subsequently collected and edited by Richard Macksey and Eugenio Donato, in *The Structuralist Controversy: The Languages of Criticism and the Sciences of Man* (1972).

47. Kristeva, 'Psychoanalysis and the Polis' (1986), 303.

48. The difficulties and anxiety which seeking to 'read' Joyce engenders is caught appositely by Jacques Derrida in his address to Joyce 'experts'

('Ulysses Gramophone') who, as Derrida puts it, call on incompetents to speak to them in order to reassure them of their authority as readers of Joyce:

> When you call on incompetents, like me, or on allegedly external competences, knowing full well that these do not exist, is it not both to humiliate them, and because you expect from these guests not only news, good news come at last to deliver you from the hypermnesic interiority in which you go round in circles like hallucinators in a nightmare, but also, paradoxically, a legitimacy? For you are at once very sure and very unsure of your rights, and even of your community, of the homogeneity of your practices, your methods, your styles. You cannot rely on the least consensus, on the least axiomatic concordat among you. As a matter of fact, you do not exist, you are not founded to exist as a foundation, which is what Joyce's signature gives you to read. And you call on strangers to come and tell you, as I am doing in replying to your invitation: you exist, you intimidate me, I recognize you, I recognize your paternal and grandpaternal authority, recognize me and give me a diploma in Joycean studies. (1992, 284)

While Derrida's reading of the situation in which he finds himself is geared specifically towards the 'community' of Joyce readers and its self-legitimating practices, the commentary nonetheless provides a pertinent analysis of the situation of reading in and by institutional structures and identities, where there is a constant negotiation concerning how 'practices', 'methods', 'styles' of reading are signed, authorised, and guaranteed.

In 'Two Words for Joyce' (1984), Derrida has commented on the impossibility of finding the right speed for reading *Finnegans Wake*, and, indeed on reading and its impossibility:

> But I'm not sure that one can say 'reading Joyce' as I just have. Of course, one can do nothing but that, whether one knows it or not. But the utterances 'I am reading Joyce', 'read Joyce', 'have you read Joyce?' produce an irresistible effect of naivety, irresistibly comical. What exactly do you mean by 'read Joyce'? Who can pride himself on having 'read Joyce'?
>
> With this admiring resentment, you stay on the edge of reading Joyce – for me this has been going on for twenty-five or thirty years – and the endless plunge throws you back onto the river-bank, on the brink of another possible immersion, *ad infinitum*. Is this true to the same extent of all works? In any case, I have the feeling that I haven't yet begun to read Joyce, and this 'not having begun to read' is sometimes the singular and active relationship I have with this work. (1984, 148)

Derrida's commentary, at once playful *and* cautious, serves as a useful corrective to Lacan's throwaway, yet imperious parenthesis (itself comical) that we 'read *Finnegans Wake*'. For Derrida, however, the question of reading *Finnegans Wake* is marked by a desire to translate: 'reading itself consists, from its very first movement, in sketching out translation' (1984, 154).

Stephen Heath sums up the difficulties in 'reading' the *Wake*:

> Reading Joyce remains a problem. This can be seen easily enough from the two rigorously complementary poles of critical reaction to *Finnegans Wake*: the

first, faced with the specific practice of writing in Joyce's text and thus with the impossibility of converting that text into a critical object, rejects it as 'aberration'; the second, seeking to preserve Joyce's text for criticism, finds itself obliged to that end to 'reduce' its writing to the simple carrier of a message (a meaning) that it will be the critic's task to 'extract from its enigmatic envelope' ... The writing [of the *Wake*] opens out onto a multiplicity of fragments of sense, of possibilities, which are traced and retraced, colliding and breaking ceaselessly in the play of this text that resists any homogenization ... *Finnegans Wake* is the space of a writing-reading. (1984, 31–2)

While *Finnegans Wake* presents us with the problems of reading, and of defining what it means to read in particularly spectacular, not to say theatrical fashion, the negotiations between reading and not reading, reading to-come and reading towards a limit which are, we might say, the reading-history of this text, are exemplary and singular instances of the contest for reading in the academy in general, and in the humanities in particular, especially since the 'beginnings' of the translation of what is termed loosely 'theory'. Thus it might be possible to seek to read the fortunes of reading, the various histories of various readings, via a reading of the reception (which is not, as we know after Nicholas Royle, the same as reading) of *Finnegans Wake* in the university (which this note has begun, albeit in a highly telegraphed fashion).

On matters of reading Joyce in the institution, and of the theoretical engagement with Joyce, see Christine van Boheemen-Saaf, 'Purloined Joyce' (1998, 246–57), and Mark Currie, 'Revisiting Poststructuralist Joyce' (1998, 258–64).

49. This remark comes from the 'Foreword' to Levinas's *Proper Names*, in which he traces a shift to an analysis which relies on the reading of textual play without the acknowledgement of a more significant resonance: 'Statements no longer succeed in putting things together'.

'Signifiers' without 'signifieds' play a 'sign game' with neither sense nor stakes. ... There is a general alienation from the meaningful as posited ... an opposition to the rigor of logical forms, adjudged to be repressive, an obsession with the inexpressible, the ineffable, the unsaid – which are sought in the awkward expression, the slip of the tongue, the scatological. Genealogy as exegesis, the dead bodies of words swollen with etymologies and devoid of *logos*, borne by the drift of the texts: such is modernity ... But a modernity that is already degenerating into elementary truths and fashionable banter. (1996, 4)

This is not simply a *caveat* against what is called 'poststructuralism'. Against the 'irresponsible' playfulness discerned, Levinas situates the proper name, as the title of the collection suggests. For Levinas, proper names offer a provisional inscription through which the Saying of the Other is projected and sustained, for proper names 'resist the dissolution of meaning' (4).

50. Levinas elaborates on the Said and the Saying in the section with that name of *Otherwise Than Being or Beyond Essence* (1998, 5–8).

The most extensive commentary on the Saying and the Said in relation to reading and the question of ethics is Simon Critchley's (1992, 30–1, 123–30, 162–82, 229–36).

Susan A. Handleman offers the following succinct interpretation:

> In *Otherwise Than Being* (1974) Levinas ... refines and radicalizes his idea of language and changes his emphasis from the 'face' to what he calls the relation of the 'saying and the said' (*le dire et le dit*). This change is partially in response to the Derridean problem of finding or articulating the 'other' of language in language. 'Saying' is still a linguistic metaphor to describe this 'other' realm, thus acknowledging the complexity of our access to it. Levinas then analyzes the oscillation between the saying and the said as the very alternation between skepticism and philosophy. 'Saying' is a 'language before language,' prior to ontology, 'origin' and representation, an-archic – and so unknowable, or prior to philosophic consciousness. But this 'saying' necessarily shows and 'betrays itself' into the 'said' – the realm of language as the set of signs which doubles being, which re-presents, synchronizes, names, designates, and which 'consciousness' grasps, manipulates, thematizes, brings to light, remembers, and in which we discuss and define this 'saying'.
>
> Levinas admits the methodological problem: the said is necessary, but it betrays the saying, and the otherwise than being becomes absorbed into being and thematization. But the task of philosophy becomes clear just at this crux: it is the necessity of continually *unsaying* the said. (1991, 233)

Another pertinent analysis is offered more recently by Jill Robbins, whose discussion makes more explicit the relationship between Levinasian ethics and the literary, which relationship she opens partly through the close analysis of Levinas's own frequent citations of literary texts (1999, 144–6). The problem of speaking about the Saying, as Robbins suggests, is that we think we know too easily what Saying is, and in treating it in this manner, we thematise it, reducing it to the said.

51. Levinas, *Proper Names* (1996), 6. In this essay on Derrida, Levinas provides another telling commentary on the relation between Saying and Said. Speaking of difference, and referring to *Speech and Phenomena*, Levinas remarks:

> What remains constructed after deconstruction is, to be sure, the stern architecture of the discourse that deconstructs and uses the verb 'to be' in the present tense in predicative statements. A discourse in the course of which, amidst the quaking of truth's underpinnings and in opposition to the self-evidence of the lived presence, which seems to offer presence a last refuge. Derrida still has the strength to utter: 'Is this certain?' As if anything could be certain at that point, and as if certainty or uncertainty should still matter.
>
> One might be tempted to draw an argument from this recourse to logocentric language in opposing that very language, in order to question the validity of the deconstruction thus produced. That is a course that has frequently been followed in refuting skepticism; but the latter ... would right itself and return as philosophy's legitimate child ...
>
> But in pursuing that course, we would risk missing the significance of that very inconsistency. We would miss the incompressible non-simultaneity of the Said and the Saying, the discrepancy in their correlation: a very slight

discrepancy, but wide enough for the discourse of skepticism to creep into it without being choked off by the contradiction between what its *said* means and the meaning of the very fact of uttering a *said*. It is as if the two meanings lacked the simultaneity that would be required for contradiction to sunder their connection. It is as if the correlation of the *Saying* and the *Said* were a diachrony of the unassemblable; and as if the situation of the Saying were already, for the Said, a 'retention memory,' but without the lapse of the instants of the Saying letting themselves be recovered in this memory. (1996, 58–9)

Levinas's articulation of the nature of difference in terms of the Saying and the Said is instructive. His reading attends to that *incompressible non-simultaneity*, an aporetic moment re-presented through the opening effected by reading. His reading opens the slightest dislocation in movement, or rather the motion of difference which makes plain, which articulates, the discrepancy or disjunction, which is neither to be recovered, closed up, nor to slip into a *simultaneity* readable simply as contradiction.

Simon Critchley has provided another translation of this essay (Levinas, 1991). In the interests of comparison, and in opening this passage to itself, we reproduce the passage from Critchley's version:

> What remains constructed after the deconstruction is, certainly, the stern architecture of the deconstructing discourse which employs the present tense of the verb 'to be' in predicative propositions. Discourse in the course of which, amidst the shaking of the foundations of truth, against the self-evidence of present lived experience which seems to offer an ultimate refuge to presence, Derrida still has the strength to say 'is this certain?' as if anything could be secure at that moment and as if security and insecurity should still matter.
>
> One might well be tempted to infer an argument from this use of logo-centric language against that very language, in order to dispute the produced deconstruction: a path much followed by the refutation of skepticism, but where, ... skepticism got back up on its feet to come back as the legitimate child of philosophy.
>
> But, in following this path, one would risk missing one side of the signifi-cation which this very inconsequence bears. One would risk missing the incompressible nonsimultaneity of the Said and the Saying, the dislocation of their correlation. A dislocation which, though minimal, would be wide enough to swallow up skeptical discourse, but without stifling itself in the contradiction between what is signified by its Said and what is signified by the very fact of articulating a Said. As if simultaneity were lacking from the two significations, so that the contradiction broke the knot that tied them together. As if the correlation of the Saying and the Said was a diachrony of that which can't be brought together (*l'inassemblable*). As if the situation of the Saying was already a 'memory retention' for the Said, but without the *lapse* of the instants of the Saying letting themselves be recuperated in this memory. (Levinas, 1991, 5–6)

Derrida has responded to Levinas's essay, in 'At this very Moment in this Work Here I Am' (1991, 11–48), exposing the *incompressible non-simultaneity* as that which does not so much inhabit the text, as it 'haunts it' (18). In response to Levinas's attention to the operation of the verb 'to be', Derrida traces the iterable disjunction in the text of Levinas through following the reiterated phrase 'here I am', which, far from grounding the text through the intimation of a voice or presence, opens it to itself through the undecidability of the phrase.

52. On the size of the ear's opening, on listening, and reception particularly in relation to teaching and its institutions, in response to Nietzsche, see, for example, Jacques Derrida's 'Otobiographies: The Teaching of Nietzsche and the Politics of the Proper Name' in *The Ear of the Other* (1988, 3–38).

53. James Joyce offers a consideration of the chance of reading as listening rather than looking in *Ulysses*. As Stephen walks across the beach, he seeks to read his movement through space and time by closing his eyes to the 'ineluctable modality of the visible':

> Ineluctable modality of the visible: at least that if no more, thought through my eyes. Signatures of all things I am here to read, seaspawn and seawrack, the nearing tide, that rusty boot. Snotgreen, bluesilver, rust: coloured signs. Limits of the diaphane ... Shut your eyes and see.
>
> Stephen closed his eyes to hear his boots crush crackling wrack and shells. You are walking through it howsomever. I am, a stride at a time. A very short space of time through very short times of space. Five, six: the *nacheinander*. Exactly: and that is the ineluctable modality of the audible. ... My two feet in his boots are at the end of his legs, *nebeneinander*. Sounds solid ... Am I walking into eternity along Sandymount strand? Crush, crack, crick, crick. Wild sea money. Dominic Deasy kens them a'.
>> *Won't you come to Sandymount,*
>> *Madeline the mare?*
> Rhythm begins you see. I hear. A catalectic tetrameter of iambs marching. No, agallop: *deline the mare*. (1993, 37)

As Stephen progresses, so the passage moves towards a more closely focused consideration of the movement of reading, so that walking, listening, and reading come to stuff, as it were, each other's function. At the same time, or nearly the same time, the problem of reading becomes more pronounced. There is, for example, some question as to whether Joyce intended 'acatalectic' or 'a catalectic' (see the 'errata' and notes to the 1993 edition of Ulysses; 748–9, 784–5). The Gabler edition (1986) goes for 'acatalectic'. Whichever might be correct, however, it is a matter of some irony that the concern over an unresolvable matter of reading should arise around a question of poetic feet, and Joyce's shift from Stephen's 'reading' of both the movement of his own feet and the sounds that issue from his steps, which, in turn, sign the text for the reader to follow, to a matter of poetic 'feet', and the question of rhythm in relation to reading. Interestingly, the matter refuses to be settled, while reading is suspended, opening itself onto the undecidable, in the very last word of the paragraph: *mare*. While we see one word, simply, and so are tempted to break off from reading in that moment, we hear, in more than one language, mother, sea, horse (sea-horse? see horse?), all of which are of significance in *Ulysses*. (Unless, of course, this is simply, on Joyce's part, a *throwaway*.) All at once, we encounter what Peggy Kamuf describes as the 'divided, suspended trait of reading *in* the text and *of* the text … [which] doubles every mark, at every step. This is what one has to read and at the same time that is what one cannot read'. Such doubling steps, whether on a beach near Dublin or Saintes-Maries-de-la-Mer, leave us with undecidable remains. Is it not possible to propose a reading of *Ulysses*, which addresses reading's impossibility, and the confrontation with the very limit of acts of reading in *Ulysses*, which would issue from this ruinous word, *mare*, and all its remains, which are found in ruins, everywhere, throughout Joyce's text? And might we not call this 'reading' 'One Word for Joyce'? Or is it already too late, is it always too late?

54. Bennington (1993), 56.
55. To the extent that the 'literary' is read or, at least, observed, as though bird-watching or train-spotting had somehow displaced reading, reading begins to come to a halt or avoided. It is often the case that the 'literary' is recognised, or 'literary' effects are identified, in what we call 'theory', 'criticism', 'philosophy', or some other manifestation of academic discourse, only to discount the work of the 'literary'. The passage of Avital Ronell's is clearly 'autobiographical', if not 'literary', and therefore confronts the question of critical reading directly through its recourse to narrative and the figural. Put simply, how are we to read a passage which departs so markedly from the conventions of critical writing in order to confront the very limits of what critical reading and writing is supposed to do?

An example of discounting a text in part because of its 'literary tendencies', or, at least, excusing oneself from reading the 'literary', is to be found in an essay by Aijaz Ahmad, 'Reconciling Derrida: "Specters of Marx" and Deconstructive Politics' (1999, 88-109). One passage in particular announces Derrida's 'literariness', thereby discounting Derrida's text, and excusing Ahmad from reading:

> The first question that arises, of course, is: what *kind* of text is it that Derrida has composed? Considering the plenitude of motifs and metaphors, and considering also the centrality of the *form* of rhetoric for the affects and effectivity of this text, one would be inclined to treat it primarily as a *literary* text. This literary quality is deeply embedded, then, in what I take to be its primary purpose, namely *performance*. We have, in other words, essentially a *performative* text in a distinctly literary mode. A text that offers not analysis but performance: a ritual performance of burial and recouping, hence the motifs of oath and spectrality and promise. (1999, 90–1)

What is all the more interesting is that this passage, which begins to conclude Ahmad's introduction, follows immediately on from his own attention to the semantics, if not the 'literary' of figural effects, of his choice of the word 'reconciling' in his title, where the possible operations of that word, and subsequent readings, are played out in explanation of his argument. However, that aside, considering the gambit by which Ahmad situates himself and his kind of Marxism (90), that of raising the question of what *kind* of text *Specters of Marx* is, one would be inclined to treat Ahmad's postulation as primarily rhetorical rather than analytical. This rhetorical quality is deeply embedded, then, in what I take to be its primary purpose, which is to avoid reading. This is announced in the assertion that it is performance, rather than analysis, which is offered, as though the two were so easily separable and distinct as though, for example, the rhetorical question had no role in political, or politicised analysis.

In 'Marx & Sons' Derrida responds to Ahmad's comment in the following fashion:

> Ahmad is right, it seems to me, to wonder, 'what *kind* of a text is it that Derrida has composed?' Indeed, one understands nothing about this text if one fails to take into account the specificity of its gesture, its writing, composition, rhetoric and address – in a word, everything a traditional reader in a rush would have called its form, or tone, but which I, for my part, consider inseparable from its content. Ahmad is right again when, answering his very good question, he says: 'We have, in other words, essentially a *performative* text …' Yes, of course. But I am, naturally, no longer in agreement with him when he reduces this performativity to a 'performance', especially to the 'performance' of a 'literary text', especially when this 'performance' is in its turn reduced to conventional, confused notions of 'form of rhetoric', 'affectivity', 'tone', and so forth. Who would deny that there are rhetoric, affect and tone in *Specters of Marx*? I certainly would not; but I lay a different kind of claim to them, and relate them differently to the performativity of the analysis itself. Does Aijaz Ahmad think his text is so very atonal? Does he think that what he writes has been purged of all affectivity, all rhetoric, and since this too is a matter that seems to bother him, of every gesture of 'filiation and affiliation'? (1999, 230)

The debate here is very much one concerned with the extent to which one allows oneself to be open to reading. Ahmad's rhetorical accusation of Derrida's literariness belongs to, and performs with all the effects of, that kind of politicised reading-within-limits of which Geoffrey Bennington speaks in the fragment of '*Inter*' presented above. In Aijaz Ahmad's discussion, the impatience of the *reading-towards-socialism*, which excuses itself from reading – except when it suits it – is made clear, while Derrida's text, in being literary is prejudged or presupposed as being *not political **enough**, never political enough*.

56. Iain Sinclair (1997), 2.
57. *Provenance*, taken to mean simply discernible origin or derivation, names also that which is to come out, that which moves forward or onward, that which is away from its place, while also being articulated in part by the future and that which is to-come, in its partial citation of *venir*.
58. The following is taken from Kamuf's introduction to her *A Derrida Reader: Between the Blinds* (1991), xiv–xv.
59. We find the impossibility of assigning an authoritative beginning remarked

here, in this case whether we are interested in the *private place* of Pepys, as identified by Francis Barker, or the *scenes of solitude*, beginning with Augustine's silent reading noted by Stewart.

60. The dates refer to the publication of Roland Barthes's *Mythologies*, first in French and then, for the first time, again, in English.

61. We cannot take time for the reason Derrida explains in *Given Time*:

> What is it *to have time?* If a time belongs, it is because the word *time* designates metonymically less time itself than the things with which one fills it, with which one fills the form of time, time *as form*. It is a matter, then, of the things one does *in the meantime* [cependant] or the things one has at one's disposal *during* [pendant] this time. Therefore, as time does not belong to anyone as such, one can no more *take* it, itself, than *give* it. Time already begins to appear as that which undoes this distinction between taking and giving, therefore also between receiving and giving, perhaps between receptivity and activity, or even between the being-affected and the affecting of any affection. Apparently and according to common logic or economics, one can only exchange, one can only take or give, by way of metonymy, what is *in* time. (1992, 3)

Works Cited

Ahmad, Aijaz. 'Reconciling Derrida: 'Specters of Marx' and Deconstructive Politics'. [1994] *Ghostly Demarcations: A Symposium on Jacques Derrida's Specters of Marx*. Ed. Michael Sprinker. London: Verso, 1999, 88–109.

Althusser, Louis, and Etienne Balibar. *Reading Capital*. [1968] Trans. Ben Brewster. London: Verso, 1979.

Barker, Francis. *The Tremulous Private Body: Essays on Subjection*. London: Methuen, 1984.

Barthes, Roland. *Mythologies*. [1957] Trans. Annette Lavers. New York: Hill and Wang, 1995.

Barthes, Roland. *S/Z*. [1970] Trans. Richard Miller, Preface Richard Howard. New York: Farrar, Strauss and Giroux, 1974.

Barthes, Roland. 'Where to Begin?' *New Critical Essays*. [1972] Trans. Richard Howard. Berkeley and Los Angeles: University of California Press, 1990, 79–91.

Baudelaire, Charles. 'Le Peintre de la vie moderne'. *L'Art romantique, Œuvres complètes*. Vol. IV. Ed. F. F. Gauthier. Paris: n.p., 1923. Trans. as 'The Painter of Modern Life'. Trans. P. E. Charvet. In Charles Baudelaire, *Selected Writings on Art and Literature*. Trans. and int. P. E. Charvet. London: Penguin, 1992, 390–436.

Beardsworth, Richard. *Derrida and the Political*. London: Routledge, 1996.

Belay, Boris. 'Translating Istrice'. *The French Connections of Jacques Derrida*. Ed. Julian Wolfreys, John Brannigan, and Ruth Robbins. New York: State University of New York Press, 1999, 165–74.

Bennington, Geoffrey. 'Demanding History'. [1983] *Legislations: The Politics of Deconstruction*. London: Verso, 1994, 61–73.

Bennington, Geoffrey. 'Derridabase'. Trans. Geoffrey Bennington. In Geoffrey Bennington and Jacques Derrida, *Jacques Derrida*. [1991] Chicago: University of Chicago Press, 1993, 3–316.

Bennington, Geoffrey. 'Inter'. *Post-Theory: New Directions in Criticism*. Ed. Martin McQuillan, Graeme MacDonald, Robin Purves, and Stephen Thomson. Edinburgh: Edinburgh University Press, 1999, 103–19.

Bennington, Geoffrey. 'Not Yet'. [1981] *Legislations: The Politics of Deconstruction*. London: Verso, 1994, 74–87.

Bennington, Geoffrey. 'Outside Story'. [1983] *Legislations: The Politics of Deconstruction*. London: Verso, 1994, 88–98.

Bennington, Geoffrey. 'X'. *Applying: To Derrida*. Ed. John Brannigan, Ruth Robbins, Julian Wolfreys. Basingstoke: Macmillan, 1996, 1–20.

Bhabha, Homi K. 'The Commitment to Theory'. *The Location of Culture*. London: Routledge, 1994, 19–39.

Bloom, Harold. *The Anxiety of Influence*. New York: Oxford University Press, 1973.

Butler, Judith. *Bodies that Matter: On the Discursive Limits of 'Sex'*. New York: Routledge, 1993.

Cascardi, Anthony J. *Consequences of Enlightenment*. Cambridge: Cambridge University Press, 1999.

Cixous, Hélène. *Three Steps on the Ladder of Writing*. Trans. Sarah Cornell and Susan Sellers. New York: Columbia University Press, 1993.

Cixous, Hélène. 'Without end, no, State of drawingness, no, rather: The Executioner's taking off'. [1991] Trans. Catherine A. F. MacGillivray. In Hélène Cixous, *Stigmata: Escaping Texts*. London: Routledge, 1998, 20–31.

Clark, Timothy. *Derrida, Heidegger, Blanchot: Sources of Derrida's Notion and Practice of Literature*. Cambridge: Cambridge University Press, 1992.

Cornell, Drucilla. *The Philosophy of the Limit*. New York: Routledge, 1992.

Critchley, Simon. *The Ethics of Deconstruction: Derrida and Levinas*. Oxford: Blackwell, 1992.

Critchley, Simon. *Very Little … Almost Nothing: Death, Philosophy, Literature*. London: Routledge, 1997.

Currie, Mark. 'Revisiting Poststructuralist Joyce'. *Re: Joyce. Text • Culture • Politics*. Ed. John Brannigan, Geoff Ward, Julian Wolfreys. Basingstoke: Macmillan, 1998, 258–64.

de Bolla, Peter. *The Discourse of the Sublime: History, Aesthetics and the Subject*. Oxford: Basil Blackwell, 1989.

de Man, Paul. *Blindness and Insight*. Oxford: Oxford University Press, 1971.

de Man, Paul. *The Resistance to Theory*. Foreword Wlad Godzich. Minneapolis: University of Minnesota Press, 1986.

de Man, Paul. *The Rhetoric of Romanticism*. New York: Columbia University Press, 1984.

Derrida, Jacques. 'Acts: The Meaning of a Given Word'. [1986] Trans. Eduardo Cadava. *Mémoires for Paul de Man*. Rev. Ed. Trans. Cecile Lindsay et al. New York: Columbia University Press, 1989, 89–154.

Derrida, Jacques. 'Afterw.rds or, at least, less than a letter about a letter less'. *Afterwords*. Ed. Nicholas Royle. Tampere: Outside Books, 1992, 197–203.

Derrida, Jacques. 'Aphorism Countertime'. [1986] Trans. Nicholas Royle. Jacques Derrida, *Acts of Literature*. Ed. Derek Attridge. New York: Routledge, 1992, 411–33.

Derrida, Jacques. 'The Art of *Mémoires*'. [1986] Trans. Jonathan Culler. *Mémoires for Paul de Man*. Rev. Ed. Trans. Cecile Lindsay et al. New York: Columbia University Press, 1989, 45–88.

Derrida, Jacques. ' "*As if* I Were Dead": An Interview with Jacques Derrida'. *Applying: To Derrida*. Ed. John Brannigan, Ruth Robbins, and Julian Wolfreys. Basingstoke: Macmillan, 1996, 212–26.

Derrida, Jacques. 'At this very Moment in this Work Here I Am'. Trans. Ruben Berezdivin. *Re-Reading Levinas*. Ed. Robert Bernasconi and Simon Critchley. Bloomington: Indiana University Press, 1991, 11–48.

Derrida, Jacques. 'Border Lines'. Trans. James Hulbert. In Harold Bloom et al., *Deconstruction and Criticism*. New York: Continuum, 1979, 75–176.

Derrida, Jacques. 'Che cos'è la poesia?' Trans. P. Kamuf [1988] *A Derrida Reader: Between the Blinds*. Ed. Peggy Kamuf. New York: Columbia University Press, 1991, 222–37.

Derrida, Jacques. *Dissemination*. [1972] Trans. and int. Barbara Johnson. Chicago: University of Chicago Press, 1981.

Derrida, Jacques. *The Ear of the Other.* [1985] Ed. Christie McDonald. Trans. Peggy Kamuf and Avital Ronell. Lincoln: University of Nebraska Press, 1988.

Derrida, Jacques. 'Fifty-Two Aphorisms for a Foreword'. *Deconstruction: Omnibus Volume*. Ed. Andreas Papdakis, Catherine Cooke, and Andrew Benjamin. London: Academy Editions, 1989, 67–9.

Derrida, Jacques. 'Force and Signification'. [1967] *Writing and Difference*. Trans. and int. Alan Bass. Chicago: University of Chicago Press, 1978, 3–30.

Derrida, Jacques. *Given Time: I. Counterfeit Money*. Trans. Peggy Kamuf. Chicago: University of Chicago Press, 1992.

Derrida, Jacques. *Glas*. [1974] Trans. John P. Leavey, Jr., and Richard Rand. Lincoln: University of Nebraska Press, 1986.

Derrida, Jacques. '*Honoris Causa:* "This Is *also* extremely funny" '. Trans. Marion Hobson and Christopher Johnson. *Points ... Interviews, 1974–1994*. [1992] Ed. Elisabeth Weber. Trans. Peggy Kamuf et al. Stanford: Stanford University Press, 1995, 399–421.

Derrida, Jacques. 'Letter to a Japanese Friend'. [1983] *A Derrida Reader: Between the Blinds*. Ed. Peggy Kamuf. New York: Columbia University Press, 1991, 270–6.

Derrida, Jacques. *Margins of Philosophy*. [1972] Trans. Alan Bass. Chicago: University of Chicago Press, 1982.

Derrida, Jacques. 'Marx & Sons'. Trans. G. M. Goshgarian. *Ghostly Demarcations: A Symposium on Jacques Derrida's* Specters of Marx. Ed. Michael Sprinker. London: Verso, 1999, 213–69.

Derrida, Jacques. *Of Grammatology*. [1967] Trans. Gayatri Chakravorty Spivak. Baltimore: The Johns Hopkins University Press, 1976.

Derrida, Jacques, 'Politics and Friendship: An Interview with Jacques Derrida'. Trans. Robert Harvey. *The Althusserian Legacy*. Ed. E. Ann Kaplan and Michael Sprinker. London: Verso, 1993, 183–232.

Derrida, Jacques. *The Post Card: From Socrates to Freud and Beyond*. [1980] Trans. Alan Bass. Chicago: University of Chicago Press, 1987.

Derrida, Jacques. 'The *Retrait* of Metaphor'. [1978] Trans. F. Gasdner. *Enclitic*, 2:2 (1987), 5–33. Rpt in Julian Wolfreys (ed.), *The Derrida Reader: Writing*

Performances. Edinburgh: Edinburgh University Press, 1998, 102–29.

Derrida, Jacques. *Right of Inspection*. [1985] Photographs by Marie-Françoise Plissart. Trans. David Wills. New York: Monacelli Press, 1998.

Derrida, Jacques. 'Some Statements and Truisms about Neologisms, Newisms, Postisms, Parasitisms, and Other Small Seismisms'. Trans. Anne Tomiche. *The States of 'Theory': History, Art, and Critical Discourse*. Ed. David Carroll. New York: Columbia University Press, 1990, 63–94.

Derrida, Jacques. 'Two Words for Joyce'. Trans. Geoff Bennington. *Post-Structuralist Joyce: Essays from the French*. Ed. Derek Attridge and Daniel Ferrer. Cambridge: Cambridge University Press, 1984, 145–59.

Derrida, Jacques. 'Ulysses Gramophone: Hear Say Yes in Joyce'. [1987] Trans. Tina Kendall, rev. Shari Benstock. Jacques Derrida, *Acts of Literature*. Ed. Derek Attridge. New York: Routledge, 1992, 253–309.

Felman, Shoshana. *What Does a Woman Want? Reading and Sexual Difference*. Baltimore: Johns Hopkins, 1993.

Foucault, Michel. 'Self Writing'. Trans. Paul Rabinow. *Ethics: The Essential Works 1*. [1994] Ed. Paul Rabinow. London: Penguin, 1997, 207-22.

Frey, Hans-Jost. *Interruptions*. [1989] Trans. Georgia Albert. Albany: State University of New York Press, 1996.

Hamacher, Werner. *Pleroma: Reading in Hegel*. [1978] Trans. Nicholas Walker and Simon Jarvis. Stanford: Stanford University Press, 1998.

Handleman, Susan A. *Fragments of Redemption: Jewish Thought and Literary Theory in Benjamin, Scholem, and Levinas*. Bloomington: Indiana University Press, 1991.

Heath, Stephen. 'Ambiviolences: Notes for Reading Joyce'. *Post-Structuralist Joyce: Essays from the French*. Ed. Derek Attridge and Daniel Ferrer. Cambridge: Cambridge University Press, 1984, 31–68.

Heidegger, Martin. 'The End of Philosophy and the Task of Thinking'. [1966] Trans. Joan Stambaugh. *Basic Writings: Revised and Expanded Edition*. Ed. David Farrell Krell. London: Routledge, 1993, 431–49.

Heidegger, Martin. *Poetry, Language, Thought*. Trans. and int. Albert Hofstadter. New York: Harper and Row, 1971.

Irigaray, Luce. *The Forgetting of Air in Martin Heidegger*. [1983] Trans. Mary Beth Mader. Austin: University of Texas Press, 1999.

Joyce, James. *Ulysses*. [1922] Ed. Hans Walter Gabler et al. London: The Bodley Head, 1986.

Joyce, James. *Ulysses*. [1922] Ed. Jeri Johnson. Oxford: Oxford University Press, 1993.

Kamuf, Peggy. *The Division | of Literature or the University in Deconstruction*. Chicago: University of Chicago Press, 1997.

Kamuf, Peggy. 'Introduction: Reading Between the Blinds'. *A Derrida Reader: Between the Blinds*. Ed. Peggy Kamuf. New York: Columbia University Press, 1991, xii–xlii.

Keenan, Dennis King. *Death and Responsibility: The 'Work' of Levinas*. Albany: State University of New York Press, 1999.

Keenan, Thomas. *Fables of Responsibility: Aberrations and Predicaments in Ethics and*

Politics. Stanford: Stanford University Press, 1997.

Kofman, Sarah. *Nietzsche and Metaphor*. [1972] Trans. Duncan Large. London: Athlone Press, 1993.

Krell, David Farrell. *Infectious Nietzsche*. Bloomington: University of Indiana Press, 1996.

Kristeva, Julia. 'Psychoanalysis and the Polis'. [1982] Trans. Margaret Waller. *The Kristeva Reader*. Ed. Toril Moi. Oxford: Blackwell, 1986, 301–20.

Kristeva, Julia. *Séméiotiké: Recherches pour une sémanalyse*. Paris: Seuil, 1969.

Kristeva, Julia. 'Semiotics: A Critical Science and/or a Critique of Science'. [1968] Trans. Seán Hand. *The Kristeva Reader*. Ed. Toril Moi. Oxford: Blackwell, 1986, 74–88.

Kristeva, Julia. 'Word, Dialogue and Novel'. [1966] Trans. Seán Hand. *The Kristeva Reader*. Ed. Toril Moi. Oxford: Blackwell, 1986, 34–61.

Lacan, Jacques. 'The Function of the Written'. *The Seminar of Jacques Lacan: On Feminine Sexuality, The Limits of Love and Knowledge Book XX Encore 1972–1973*. [1975] Ed. Jacques-Alain Miller. Trans. Bruce Fink. New York: Norton, 1998.

Lacoue-Labarthe, Philippe. *Typography: Mimesis, Philosophy, Politics*. Int. Jacques Derrida. Ed. Christopher Fynsk. Trans. Christopher Fynsk et al. Cambridge, MA: Harvard University Press, 1989.

Leavey, Jr., John P. 'French Kissing: Whose Tongue Is It Anyway?' *The French Connections of Jacques Derrida*. Ed. Julian Wolfreys, John Brannigan, and Ruth Robbins. Albany: State University of New York Press, 1999, 149–63.

Levinas, Emmanuel. *Basic Philosophical Writings*. Ed. Adriaan T. Peperzak, Simon Critchley, and Robert Bernasconi. Bloomington: Indiana University Press, 1996.

Levinas, Emmanuel. *Beyond the Verse: Talmudic Readings and Lectures*. [1982] Trans. Gary D. Mole. Bloomington: Indiana University Press, 1994.

Levinas, Emmanuel. *Ethics and Infinity: Conversations with Philippe Nemo*. [1982] Trans. Richard A. Cohen. Pittsburgh: Duquesne University Press, 1985.

Levinas, Emmanuel. *Otherwise Than Being or Beyond Essence*. [1974] Trans. Alphonso Lingis. Pittsburgh: Duquesne University Press, 1998.

Levinas, Emmanuel. *Proper Names*. [1976] Trans. Michael B. Smith. Stanford: Stanford University Press, 1996.

Levinas, Emmanuel. 'There Is: Existence without Existents'. [1946] Trans. Alphonso Lingis. *The Levinas Reader*. Ed. Seán Hand. Oxford: Blackwell, 1994. 29–36.

Levinas, Emmanuel. *Time and the Other (and Additional Essays)*. [1947, 1979] Trans. Richard A. Cohen. Pittsburgh: Duquesne University Press, 1987.

Levinas, Emmanuel. *Totality and Infinity: An Essay on Exteriority*. [1961] Trans. Alphonso Lingis. Pittsburgh: Duquesne University Press, 1969.

Levinas, Emmanuel. 'Wholly Otherwise'. [1976] Trans. Simon Critchley. *Re-Reading Levinas*. Ed. Robert Bernasconi and Simon Critchley. Bloomington: Indiana University Press, 1991, 3–10.

Lyotard, Jean-François. *The Postmodern Explained*. [1988] Ed. Julian Pefanis and

Morgan Thomas. Trans. Don Barry, Bernadette Maher, Julian Pefanis, Virginia Spate, and Morgan Thomas. Afterword Wlad Godzich. Minneapolis: University of Minnesota Press, 1992.

Malik, Suhail. 'Différantial Technics'. *Imprimatur.* 1:2/3 [1996], 200–3.

Mill, John Stuart. *On Liberty.* [1859] *On Liberty and Other Essays.* Ed. John Gray. Oxford: Oxford University Press, 1991.

Miller, J. Hillis. *The Ethics of Reading: Kant, de Man, Eliot, Trollope, James, and Benjamin.* New York: Columbia University Press, 1987.

Nägele, Rainer. *Echoes of Translation: Reading Between Texts.* Baltimore: Johns Hopkins, 1997.

Nancy, Jean-Luc. *The Birth to Presence.* Trans. Brian Holmes et al. Stanford: Stanford University Press, 1993.

Nancy, Jean-Luc. *The Sense of the World.* [1993] Trans. and Foreword Jeffrey S. Librett. Minneapolis: University of Minnesota Press, 1997.

Peperzak, Adriaan T. 'Preface'. In Emmanuel Levinas, *Basic Philosophical Writings,* 1996, vii–xv.

Pepper, Thomas. *Singularities: Extremes of Theory in the Twentieth Century.* Cambridge: Cambridge University Press, 1997.

Pepys, Samuel. *The Diary of Samuel Pepys. Volume IX 1668–1669.* [1971] Ed. Robert Latham and William Matthews. London: HarperCollins, 1995.

Plotnitsky, Arkady. 'Un-*scriptible*'. *Writing the Image after Roland Barthes.* Ed. Jean-Michel Rabaté. Philadelphia: University of Pennsylvania Press, 1997, 243–58.

Rabaté, Jean-Michel. 'Lapsus ex machina'. *Post-Structuralist Joyce: Essays from the French.* Ed. Derek Attridge and Daniel Ferrer. Trans. Elizabeth Guild. Cambridge: Cambridge University Press, 1984, 79–102.

Readings, Bill. *Introducing Lyotard: Art and Politics.* London: Routledge, 1991.

Robbins, Jill. *Altered Reading: Levinas and Literature.* Chicago: University of Chicago Press, 1999.

Ronell, Avital. *Finitude's Score: Essays for the End of the Millennium.* Lincoln: University of Nebraska Press, 1994.

Royle, Nicholas. *After Derrida.* Manchester: Manchester University Press, 1995.

Royle, Nicholas. *Telepathy and Literature: Essays on the Reading Mind.* Oxford: Blackwell, 1991.

Sartiliot, Claudette. *Citation and Modernity: Derrida, Joyce, and Brecht.* Norman: University of Oklahoma Press, 1993.

Shakespeare, William. *William Shakespeare: The Complete Works.* Ed. Stanley Wells, Gary Taylor, et al. Oxford: Oxford University Press, 1988.

Sherwood, Yvonne M. ' "White Mythology" or "Metaphor in the Text of Theology" ': Jacques Derrida among the Prophets of the Hebrew Bible'. *Imprimatur.* 1:2/3 (Spring 1996), 83–9.

Sinclair, Iain. *Lights Out for the Territory: 9 Excursions in the Secret History of London.* London: Granta, 1997.

Stewart, Susan. *On Longing: Narratives of the Miniature, the Gigantic, the Souvenir, the Collection.* Durham, NC: Duke University Press, 1993.

Tschumi, Bernard. *Architecture and Disjunction.* Cambridge, MA: MIT Press, 1994.

van Boheemen-Saaf, Christine. 'Purloined Joyce'. *Re: Joyce. Text • Culture • Politics.* Ed. John Brannigan, Geoff Ward, Julian Wolfreys. Basingstoke: Macmillan, 1998, 246–57.

Wall, Thomas Carl. *Radical Passivity: Levinas, Blanchot, and Agamben.* Albany: State University of New York Press, 1999.

Young, Robert. *White Mythologies: Writing History and the West.* London: Routledge, 1990.

Žižek, Slavoj. *The Plague of Fantasies.* London: Verso, 1997.